파고다 시험 직전 마무리 모의고사

Vol. 2

3회분

파고다교육그룹 언어교육연구소 | 저

9,900원

2018년 기출 반영
고득점 적중 600제 수록!

 모의고사 3회분
 OMR 3장
 QR코드 음원·해설
 LC 음원
 LC 스크립트
 온라인 해설서

D-3
990점 목표

PAGODA Books

파고다토익 시험 직전 마무리 모의고사 Vol. 2

TEST 1

해설 바로 보기

음원 바로 듣기

PAGODA Books

시험 진행 안내

❶ **시험 시간: 120분(2시간)**
  · Listening Comprehension 100문제: 45분
  · Reading Comprehension 100문제: 75분
  · L/C 진행 후 휴식 시간 없이 바로 R/C 진행

❷ **준비물**
  · 컴퓨터용 사인펜 또는 연필

❸ **시험 응시 준수 사항**
  · 시험 시작 10분 전 입실 (이후에는 입실 불가)
  · 종료 30분 전과 10분 전에 시험 종료 공지함
  · 휴대전화의 전원을 꺼둘 것

❹ **OMR 답안지 표기 요령**
  · 반드시 컴퓨터용 사인펜 또는 연필로 표기
  · 개인정보, 문제번호, 단체명, 문제번호, 학과(부서) 및 학번코드 표기
    (학과(부서)코드는 별도 공지)

※ 개인정보, 문제번호, 학과(부서)코드를 틀리게 표기했을 경우 채점 및 성적 확인이 불가능하므로 주의하시기 바랍니다.

답안 작성 요령 Sample
○   ● Ⓑ Ⓒ Ⓓ
×   Ⓐ Ⓑ Ⓒ̸ Ⓓ
×   Ⓐ Ⓑ Ⓒ Ⓓ
×   Ⓐ Ⓑ̸ Ⓒ Ⓓ
×   Ⓐ Ⓑ̸ Ⓒ Ⓓ

LISTENING TEST

In the Listening test, you will be asked to demonstrate how well you understand spoken English. The entire listening test will last approximately 45 minutes. There are four parts, and directions are given for each part. You must mark your answers on the separate answer sheet. Do not write your answers in your test book.

PART 1

Directions: For each question in this part, you will hear four statements about a picture in your test book. When you hear the statements, you must select the one statement that best describes what you see in the picture. Then find the number of the question on your answer sheet and mark your answer. The statements will not be printed in your test book and will be spoken only one time.

Statement (B), "A man is pointing at a document," is the best description of the picture, so you should select answer (B) and mark it on your answer sheet.

1.

2.

GO ON TO THE NEXT PAGE

3.

4.

5.

6.

PART 2

Directions: You will hear a question or statement and three responses spoken in English. They will not be printed in your test book and will be spoken only one time. Select the best response to the question or statement and mark the letter (A), (B), or (C) on your answer sheet.

7. Mark your answer on your answer sheet.
8. Mark your answer on your answer sheet.
9. Mark your answer on your answer sheet.
10. Mark your answer on your answer sheet.
11. Mark your answer on your answer sheet.
12. Mark your answer on your answer sheet.
13. Mark your answer on your answer sheet.
14. Mark your answer on your answer sheet.
15. Mark your answer on your answer sheet.
16. Mark your answer on your answer sheet.
17. Mark your answer on your answer sheet.
18. Mark your answer on your answer sheet.
19. Mark your answer on your answer sheet.
20. Mark your answer on your answer sheet.
21. Mark your answer on your answer sheet.
22. Mark your answer on your answer sheet.
23. Mark your answer on your answer sheet.
24. Mark your answer on your answer sheet.
25. Mark your answer on your answer sheet.
26. Mark your answer on your answer sheet.
27. Mark your answer on your answer sheet.
28. Mark your answer on your answer sheet.
29. Mark your answer on your answer sheet.
30. Mark your answer on your answer sheet.
31. Mark your answer on your answer sheet.

PART 3

Directions: You will hear some conversations between two or more people. You will be asked to answer three questions about what the speakers say in each conversation. Select the best response to each question and mark the letter (A), (B), (C), or (D) on your answer sheet. The conversations will not be printed in your test book and will be spoken only one time.

32. Where does the woman probably work?

(A) At a dental office
(B) At a hardware store
(C) At a landscaping firm
(D) At a real estate agency

33. What would the man like to do?

(A) Move an appointment
(B) Discuss an invoice
(C) Order a different item
(D) Return a part

34. What does the man make a recommendation about?

(A) What company to use
(B) What product to choose
(C) Which supplies to bring
(D) Which street to avoid

35. What are the speakers mainly discussing?

(A) A research project
(B) A job candidate
(C) A technical issue
(D) An award nomination

36. What does the woman explain to the man?

(A) She will evaluate some employees.
(B) She will organize a company workshop.
(C) She is planning to purchase new equipment.
(D) She is currently busy with another task.

37. Why does the man need to use the event hall today?

(A) To rehearse a speech
(B) To hold a celebration
(C) To give a tour
(D) To rearrange seating areas

38. What is the problem?

(A) There is no available equipment.
(B) A contract is missing information.
(C) A project was completed late.
(D) There is a scheduling conflict.

39. What does the man ask about?

(A) Setting up videoconferencing
(B) Changing a workshop time
(C) Installing a program
(D) Registering for an event

40. What does the woman say she will do?

(A) Get a manager's approval
(B) Email some documents
(C) Call some clients
(D) Reserve another room

41. What are the speakers mainly discussing?

(A) Their travel plans
(B) Their expense reports
(C) A subscription fee
(D) A fashion designer

42. According to the man, why has he been busy lately?

(A) He is supervising a new employee.
(B) He was recently promoted.
(C) He is working on a magazine.
(D) He transferred to another branch.

43. What does the woman offer to do for the man?

(A) Reserve a ticket
(B) Edit his work
(C) Research some venues
(D) Talk to a manager

GO ON TO THE NEXT PAGE

44. Where most likely are the speakers?

(A) At a fitness center
(B) At a grocery store
(C) At a restaurant
(D) At a library

45. What does the woman mean when she says, "This will be my first time making it"?

(A) She wishes to get some instructions.
(B) She is not sure about the quality of an item.
(C) She will ask a friend for assistance.
(D) She thinks a task will take a long time.

46. Where will the speakers most likely go next?

(A) To a storage room
(B) To a different branch
(C) To a cashier station
(D) To a guest center

47. What does the man need help doing?

(A) Registering for a seminar
(B) Accessing the Internet
(C) Making some photocopies
(D) Booking a room

48. Why does Jeanell say, "I had no problems with the computer in the Lecture Hall"?

(A) To recommend a different location
(B) To acknowledge an error
(C) To offer help on an assignment
(D) To review a procedure

49. What will the man most likely do next?

(A) Reboot a computer
(B) Review an office floor plan
(C) Visit a Web site
(D) Talk to a manager

50. Where do the speakers most likely work?

(A) At an interior design firm
(B) At a moving company
(C) At a photography studio
(D) At a magazine publisher

51. What does the man say the women will do this week?

(A) Attend a workshop
(B) Conduct some interviews
(C) Discuss an assignment
(D) Use the same office

52. What does the man ask Aaliyah?

(A) Where she placed some files
(B) When she began working at a company
(C) What kind of transportation she takes
(D) Who she suggests as a mentor

53. What kind of position did the woman apply for?

(A) Construction supervisor
(B) Travel agent
(C) Archaeologist
(D) Auditor

54. Why is the woman unsure about accepting the job?

(A) She is concerned about her qualifications.
(B) She would need to go on frequent trips.
(C) She would need to move to another town.
(D) She has received a better offer from another firm.

55. What part of the job is the man willing to discuss again?

(A) The salary figure
(B) The number of vacation days
(C) The location of the job
(D) The starting date

56. Where do the speakers most likely work?

    (A) At a nutrition store
    (B) At a medical center
    (C) At a technology company
    (D) At a health club

57. What does the woman ask about?

    (A) The length of an event
    (B) The qualifications of a candidate
    (C) The deadline for an assignment
    (D) The pricing of a service

58. What does the woman instruct the man to do?

    (A) Relay information to employees
    (B) Print out some documents
    (C) Book a meeting room
    (D) Review some job applications

59. According to the woman, what did some people complain about?

    (A) Parking spaces
    (B) Ticket prices
    (C) Food options
    (D) Booth locations

60. Why does the man say he is NOT concerned?

    (A) Notice was given in advance.
    (B) The festival was a success.
    (C) The number of attendees was high.
    (D) A deadline was met on time.

61. What does the woman suggest?

    (A) Emphasizing a policy
    (B) Providing a gift certificate
    (C) Revising a schedule
    (D) Finding a new venue

Destination terminal	Departure time
Malden	Not In Service
Garden Hills	7:55 A.M.
Woodland Green	Delays Expected
Rancho Gordo	9:10 A.M.
Malden	9:20 A.M.
Shawnee Park	10:00 A.M.

62. Look at the graphic. When will the woman's bus most likely depart?

    (A) At 7:55 A.M.
    (B) At 9:10 A.M.
    (C) At 9:20 A.M.
    (D) At 10:00 A.M.

63. What does the man ask the woman about?

    (A) Some product features
    (B) Some sales figures
    (C) Her meeting with a customer
    (D) Her participation in a training session

64. What does the man offer to do?

    (A) Inform some coworkers of a situation
    (B) Pay for the woman's transportation
    (C) Postpone a workshop
    (D) Give a presentation

GO ON TO THE NEXT PAGE

Minimum installation	
Complete installation	
Custom installation	
Trial installation	

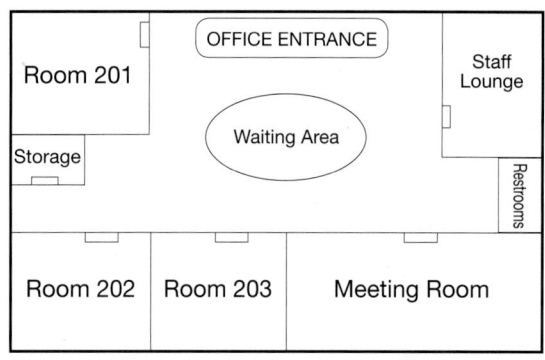

65. What does the woman say she is trying to do?

(A) Email a coworker
(B) Make a reservation
(C) Update a Web page
(D) View a file

66. Look at the graphic. Which option does the man recommend selecting?

(A) Minimum installation
(B) Complete installation
(C) Custom installation
(D) Trial installation

67. Where will the speakers most likely go next?

(A) To a product demonstration
(B) To a trade show
(C) To a company luncheon
(D) To an electronics store

68. Why has the man come to the building?

(A) To sign a contract
(B) To purchase an item
(C) To perform an installation
(D) To discuss a job opening

69. Look at the graphic. Which room will the man most likely go to?

(A) Room 201
(B) Room 202
(C) Room 203
(D) Meeting Room

70. What does the man ask to do?

(A) Store some documents
(B) Charge a device
(C) Sit in a waiting area
(D) Use a fax machine

PART 4

Directions: You will hear some talks given by a single speaker. You will be asked to answer three questions about what the speaker says in each talk. Select the best response to each question and mark the letter (A), (B), (C), or (D) on your answer sheet. The talks will not be printed in your test book and will be spoken only one time.

71. Who most likely is the speaker?

(A) A personal trainer
(B) A supermarket owner
(C) A television host
(D) A college instructor

72. What is Dr. Maray's specialty?

(A) Fitness
(B) Broadcasting
(C) Dermatology
(D) Cooking

73. What is a benefit of the product mentioned?

(A) It improves food flavors.
(B) It reduces preparation time.
(C) It promotes a healthy appetite.
(D) It minimizes infections.

74. Who most likely is the man?

(A) A computer technician
(B) A building manager
(C) A sales associate
(D) A personnel director

75. What is the man calling about?

(A) A parking permit
(B) A construction project
(C) A malfunctioning device
(D) An incorrect bill

76. Why is the woman asked to drop by an office?

(A) To pick up some mail
(B) To sign a document
(C) To make a deposit
(D) To get a new key

77. Where does the speaker most likely work?

(A) At an electronics manufacturer
(B) At a clothing retailer
(C) At an international travel agency
(D) At a vehicle rental agency

78. What problem does the speaker report?

(A) A maintenance worker is unavailable.
(B) A shipment has been delayed.
(C) A repair is required.
(D) A bill is incorrect.

79. What does the speaker offer to do?

(A) Issue a coupon
(B) Send a price list
(C) Reschedule an appointment
(D) Provide a full refund

80. Where do the listeners most likely work?

(A) At a zoo
(B) At a laboratory
(C) At a publishing firm
(D) At a manufacturing plant

81. What is Ms. Walton known for?

(A) Her grooming techniques
(B) Her social skills
(C) Her research findings
(D) Her work efficiency

82. What will Ms. Walton do this month?

(A) Take a class
(B) Receive some training
(C) Visit various branches
(D) Manage a new facility

GO ON TO THE NEXT PAGE

83. According to the speaker, what information can listeners find in a brochure?

(A) A menu
(B) A discount coupon
(C) An activity list
(D) A biography

84. Why is the event at Black Sea Eatery expected to be so popular?

(A) A well-known chef will make desserts.
(B) A live performance will be held.
(C) There were many positive reviews in the newspaper.
(D) The restaurant is opening a new location.

85. Why does the speaker say, "Black Sea Eatery doesn't accept reservations"?

(A) To propose a better venue
(B) To express disapproval of a service
(C) To recommend coming early
(D) To explain a revised policy

86. Why does the speaker say, "Not many people could have come up with such a creative idea"?

(A) He is complimenting some workers.
(B) He believes a consultant should be used.
(C) He agrees with a suggestion.
(D) He advises against continuing a project.

87. What will the company do in September?

(A) Award several employees
(B) Revise some designs
(C) Make a business deal
(D) Attend a convention

88. What does the speaker instruct the listeners to do?

(A) Inspect a machine
(B) Find a partner
(C) Turn in a form
(D) Check out a facility

89. Who most likely is the speaker?

(A) A television producer
(B) A dance instructor
(C) A musician
(D) A librarian

90. What caused a delay?

(A) Inclement weather
(B) Faulty equipment
(C) Missing baggage
(D) A late flight

91. Why does the speaker say, "we'll have a Q&A session once it's done"?

(A) To request that people do not interrupt her
(B) To recommend that listeners stay longer
(C) To explain why she will not be available
(D) To announce a schedule change

92. Who is the speaker congratulating?

(A) Advertising staff
(B) Biking professionals
(C) New clients
(D) Survey participants

93. What does the speaker say customers like about the commercial?

(A) The featured music
(B) The narrator's voice
(C) The quality of the video
(D) The scenes with athletes

94. What will the listeners probably do next week?

(A) Attend a training session
(B) Organize a race
(C) Discuss some ideas
(D) Review job applications

Sun	Mon	Tues	Wed	Thurs	Fri
17 Conference	18	19	20 Board Meeting	21	22 Supplier Negotiation

95. Look at the graphic. On which day will the speaker want to schedule the interview?

(A) Monday
(B) Tuesday
(C) Wednesday
(D) Thursday

96. What will the speaker send to Mr. Nunez?

(A) A business report
(B) A sample design
(C) A list of conference speakers
(D) A set of questions

97. What does the speaker apologize for?

(A) The date of a meeting
(B) The length of a flight
(C) The time of an interview
(D) The cost of a service

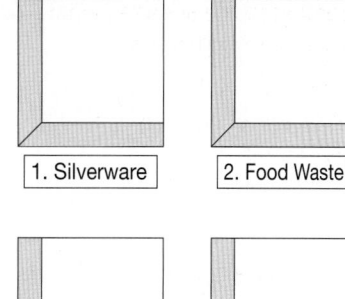
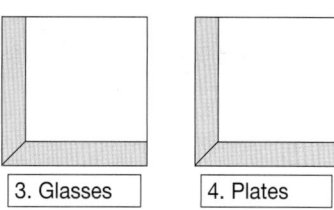

1. Silverware   2. Food Waste   3. Glasses   4. Plates

98. What does the speaker manage?

(A) An art studio
(B) A recycling plant
(C) A school cafeteria
(D) A hotel kitchen

99. Where most likely are the listeners?

(A) On a parent visit
(B) At an employee orientation
(C) At a graduation ceremony
(D) On a tour for new students

100. Look at the graphic. Which window does the speaker ask the listeners to take care with?

(A) Window 1
(B) Window 2
(C) Window 3
(D) Window 4

This is the end of the Listening test. Turn to Part 5 in your test book.

GO ON TO THE NEXT PAGE

READING TEST

In the Reading test, you will read a variety of texts and answer several different types of reading comprehension questions. The entire Reading test will last 75 minutes. There are three parts, and directions are given for each part. You are encouraged to answer as many questions as possible within the time allowed.

You must mark your answers on the separate answer sheet. Do not write your answers in your test book.

PART 5

Directions: A word or phrase is missing in each of the sentences below. Four answer choices are given below each sentence. Select the best answer to complete the sentence. Then mark the letter (A), (B), (C), or (D) on your answer sheet.

101. To prevent traffic congestion, the ------- of the Fullum Shopping Complex requires careful preparation.

    (A) constructing
    (B) construction
    (C) construct
    (D) constructive

102. When the performance is over, please exit ------- the doors on the west side of the building.

    (A) via
    (B) within
    (C) after
    (D) besides

103. ------- to the parking garage will be limited to one entrance while road repair work is being done on Paloma Street.

    (A) Accessed
    (B) Accessory
    (C) Access
    (D) Accesses

104. Selecting an effective program to design a company logo is rarely straightforward, ------- it is crucial to consult a professional designer.

    (A) then
    (B) or
    (C) so
    (D) for

105. Best-selling author Elise Darby will ------- be publishing a special collectors' edition of her novel, *Faint Hearted*.

    (A) most
    (B) soon
    (C) always
    (D) truly

106. According to the toll booth records, traffic is the lightest on the expressway ------- 3 and 5 A.M.

    (A) through
    (B) toward
    (C) during
    (D) between

107. Sales during the third quarter ------- the Marketing Department's projections.

    (A) to surpass
    (B) were surpassed
    (C) surpassing
    (D) surpassed

108. This year, Mr. Lee will start looking for new ways to ------- his own restaurant business.

    (A) finance
    (B) emerge
    (C) invest
    (D) dine

16

109. Jerome Gym's personal training courses have been in great demand -------.

(A) lately
(B) latest
(C) lateness
(D) late

110. Mr. Takihara was nominated for the Best Manager Award in ------- of his skilled negotiations during the merger.

(A) description
(B) certification
(C) recognition
(D) communication

111. Furst I&E started as a small local business but ------- transitioned into a multinational conglomerate.

(A) rather
(B) fairly
(C) greatly
(D) rapidly

112. Promotional room rates will ------- based on the monthly deals that Excar Hotel is offering.

(A) verify
(B) include
(C) differ
(D) estimate

113. The Vice President is proud to announce that ------- will create a charitable foundation for environmental protection.

(A) our
(B) us
(C) we
(D) ourselves

114. Make sure to set up a ------- number of chairs for the meeting in the afternoon.

(A) suffice
(B) sufficient
(C) sufficiently
(D) sufficing

115. The customer service center had to redirect many shipments ------- because of the unexpectedly bad weather on the coast.

(A) quicken
(B) quickest
(C) quickly
(D) quicker

116. If an incorrect order is entered into the system, it will alter not only one store's delivery schedule ------- the whole chain's.

(A) just as
(B) despite that
(C) but also
(D) such as

117. The scientists conducted supplementary experiments ------- perfect their research techniques.

(A) on account of
(B) so that
(C) in order to
(D) noticeably

118. The survey that the Public Relations Department conducted last month provided data that is ------- to our new product line.

(A) completed
(B) relevant
(C) perceptible
(D) acceptable

119. According to the Transportation Authority, the extended subway line should reduce traffic congestion in the ------- area.

(A) surrounding
(B) surround
(C) surrounds
(D) surrounded

120. The corporate guideline states that supplies, machinery, and other company ------- are not for personal use.

(A) property
(B) regulations
(C) feature
(D) matter

GO ON TO THE NEXT PAGE

121. ------- is hiring at this time of year, so recent graduates are advised to apply for jobs in January.

(A) No one
(B) Not many
(C) Anyone
(D) Any other

122. The vice president stated that there was a strong ------- the Harmer factory would be forced to cease operations.

(A) possibility
(B) possibilities
(C) possible
(D) possibly

123. ------- the government restricted the number of personal vehicles in the downtown area, the city center's parking situation has improved.

(A) Why
(B) But
(C) Since
(D) Though

124. Commuters are advised to leave their cars at home tomorrow because snowy weather -------.

(A) expects
(B) expectation
(C) is expected
(D) was expecting

125. During the renovation competition, the architects' names will be kept ------- and will be disclosed only after the winning design has been chosen.

(A) secret
(B) unique
(C) public
(D) careful

126. Ms. Park wants all meeting minutes to be typed up and emailed to the team leader ------- how trivial they may seem.

(A) aside from
(B) contrary to
(C) regardless of
(D) previous to

127. ------- quickly the construction crew may work, it will not be possible for the building to be completed within six months.

(A) Rarely
(B) However
(C) Carefully
(D) Quite

128. ------- the hotel accommodations not meet your expectations, contact the front desk to notify them of any issues.

(A) In addition to
(B) Should
(C) Anywhere
(D) Whatever

129. The employee manual contains solutions to any problems you may ------- with a client.

(A) comprise
(B) encounter
(C) qualify
(D) reside

130. Midowville has the largest ------- of automobile factories in the country.

(A) concentration
(B) recruitment
(C) convention
(D) compilation

PART 6

Directions: Read the texts that follow. A word, phrase, or sentence is missing in parts of each text. Four answer choices for each question are given below the text. Select the best answer to complete the text. Then mark the letter (A), (B), (C), or (D) on your answer sheet.

Questions 131-134 refer to the following notice.

At Malnex Industries, we take worker ------- seriously. When the forecast predicts inclement
                                        131.
weather, we carefully monitor the situation. If outside conditions pose a risk, management will close the factory.

Floor managers are in charge of informing their employees of the closures. -------. Staff
                                                                            132.
------- their normal wage for all hours that were assigned to them on the day of the closure.
133.
Once the plant is open again, everyone should return ------- for their next shift. Please direct
                                                      134.
any questions or concerns regarding these closures to your manager.

131. (A) morale
(B) benefits
(C) references
(D) safety

132. (A) The regulations are being reviewed following employee feedback.
(B) We will do our best to relay the message to our workers quickly.
(C) Management is glad that the factory does not have to close next week.
(D) It is impossible to predict inclement weather all the time.

133. (A) will earn
(B) earned
(C) had been earning
(D) have earned

134. (A) workable
(B) the work
(C) to work
(D) working

GO ON TO THE NEXT PAGE

Questions 135-138 refer to the following e-mail.

To: Arlette Moreau <arlette.m@moreaubistro.co.fr>
From: Dale Callas <dcallas@gyroworld.com>
Date: 14 March
Subject: Invitation
Attachment: brochure

Dear Ms. Moreau,

I was in the ------- during your talk at the Worldwide Entrepreneurs' Convention in Paris in February. The information you shared in your presentation on "The Value of Communication" was absolutely amazing. -------, it motivated me to reevaluate how I interact with my employees. This helped improve my relationship with my staff. Now, everyone is working more effectively. Would you be open to giving your presentation at the International Food Industry Expo in Athens in August? -------. I have attached a brochure ------- more information.

Best Regards,

Dale Callas
Owner, Gyro World

135. (A) restaurant
(B) audience
(C) vehicle
(D) country

136. (A) Meanwhile
(B) In contrast
(C) In fact
(D) Initially

137. (A) Over 2,000 experts in the industry will participate.
(B) The expo in August will probably have more attendees than the February one.
(C) This year's convention attracted more business owners.
(D) Workers in the food industry interact with customers every day.

138. (A) included those
(B) having included
(C) that includes
(D) is including

Questions 139-142 refer to the following article.

April 27 – Today, mechanical engineer Tom Winograd ------- a new business. This new
company, T. Winograd Devices, will focus on maximizing the safety and accuracy of medical
instruments. Mr. Winograd's teams of designers are experts at gathering information -------
medical records and updating technology based on patient results. -------. Mr. Winograd
believes his company's devices will be well received, saying, "We will greatly improve
doctors' potential for ------- patient satisfaction in all fields, from family medicine to surgery
and even dentistry."

139. (A) launched
(B) reviewed
(C) approached
(D) requested

140. (A) along
(B) from
(C) by
(D) to

141. (A) This technology is usually not purchased by individual patients.
(B) Most people choose clinics close to their homes or offices.
(C) Naturally, machines cannot be used as solutions to every problem.
(D) This is possible due to a special program that gathers and compares important data.

142. (A) enhancement
(B) enhance
(C) enhanced
(D) enhances

GO ON TO THE NEXT PAGE

Questions 143-146 refer to the following review.

My experience with Shaster's Home Improvement was not what I expected. Their sales associate was very polite, and he was able to get me a good discount on the sandstone bricks I purchased. However, I ------- there next time. Upon discovering some damaged
143.
pieces, I had to go back to their store. I don't think the employee checked the ------- of the
144.
bricks before he loaded them in my van. -------. Of course, the store did exchange them. In
145.
the future, I will visit a business that lets me ------- the items myself.
146.

143. (A) had been shopping
(B) might not have shopped
(C) did not shop
(D) will not be shopping

144. (A) condition
(B) price
(C) brand
(D) weight

145. (A) I decided to accept the full cash refund.
(B) The discount was only valid until last week.
(C) They were unable to fit inside my vehicle.
(D) Around a third of them could not be used.

146. (A) deliver
(B) store
(C) select
(D) return

PART 7

Directions: In this part you will read a selection of texts, such as magazine and newspaper articles, e-mails, and instant messages. Each text or set of texts is followed by several questions. Select the best answer for each question and mark the letter (A), (B), (C), or (D) on your answer sheet.

Questions 147-148 refer to the following notice.

Skyaway Air

TELL US ABOUT YOUR EXPERIENCE AND WIN A COMPLIMENTARY TRIP!

Head over to our Web site at www.skyaway.co.uk/feedback and complete the 10-minute customer satisfaction survey. You will be entered to win one of five round-trip flights to any European capital city.

All participants must be over the age of 18. Only customers who have flown with us in the last six months will be entered to win.

---

147. What is suggested about Skyaway Air?

(A) It provides discounts to children.
(B) It has partnerships with other airlines.
(C) It is planning to expand its business.
(D) It offers international flights.

148. What are customers encouraged to do?

(A) Review testimonials
(B) Book in advance
(C) Register for a membership
(D) Offer some comments

Questions 149-150 refer to the following text message chain.

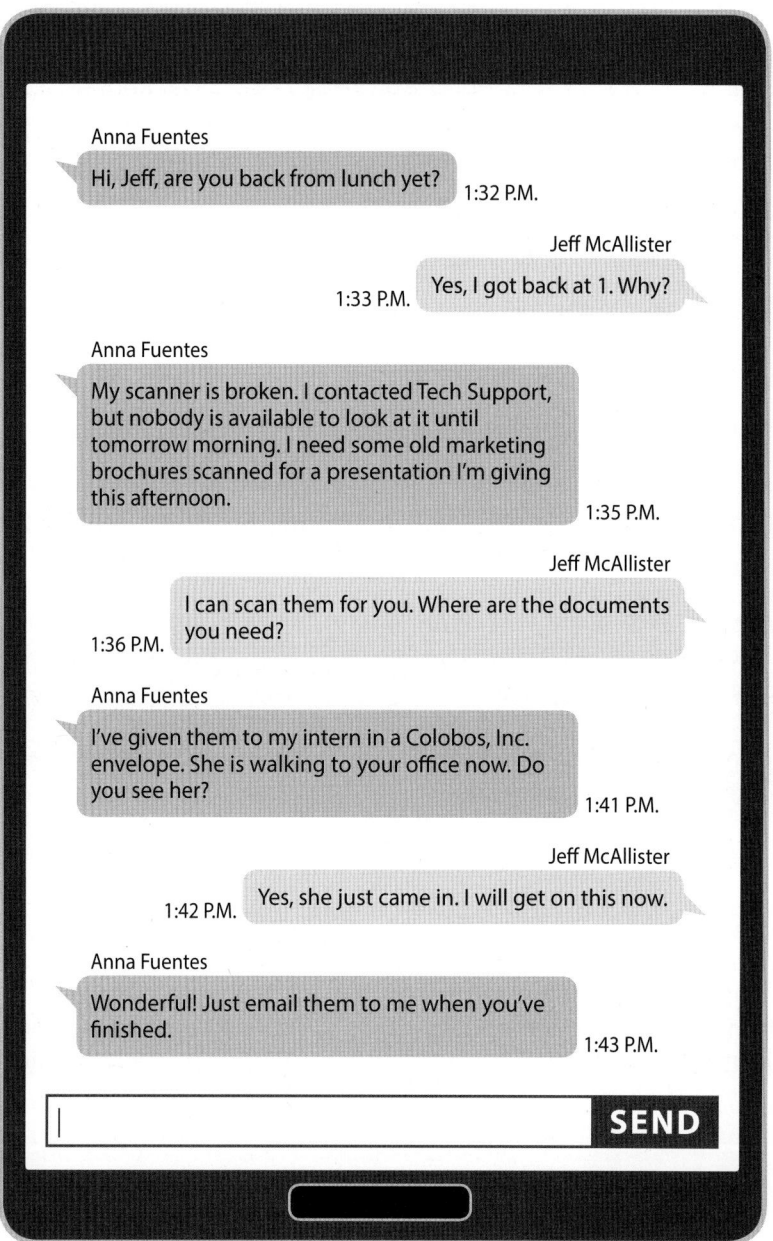

149. What problem does Ms. Fuentes mention?

(A) Some marketing materials are incorrect.
(B) Her intern is not feeling well.
(C) Some workers are not available today.
(D) A presentation will begin earlier than scheduled.

150. At 1:42 P.M., what does Mr. McAllister agree to do when he writes, "I will get on this now"?

(A) Update some files
(B) Meet a tech support employee
(C) Contact Colobos, Inc.
(D) Scan some brochures

Questions 151-152 refer to the following instructions.

Jifa Law Partners' Guidelines for Filling Out a Purchase Order Request Form

- Provide a description of the item(s), including the product code (if indicated).
- If a specific brand is needed, find the box marked "Other Brand" and write a brief summary listing your reasons.
- Include the vendor's name along with their telephone number or Web site link.
- Date and sign the form, then give it to the Accounting Department. Unsigned orders will be rejected.
- Make sure to look over your next budget report.

Note: Upon receipt of the order, the specified amount will be subtracted from your department's budget.

151. According to the instructions, what must appear on every purchase order request form?

(A) A Web site link
(B) A summary
(C) A signature
(D) A product code

152. What is indicated about the Jifa Law Partners' Accounting Department?

(A) It only allows purchases from major vendors.
(B) It provides affordable rates to Jifa Law Partners' employees.
(C) It distributes quarterly budget reports.
(D) It is able to deduct money from departmental budgets.

GO ON TO THE NEXT PAGE

Questions 153-154 refer to the following form.

Lakewood University
Parking Permit Application

1. Reason for Application
   ☐ New permit
   ☑ Lost permit

2. Personal Information
   Name: Marcus Tiller
   License Plate #: KCP-543
   State: New York
   Parking Location: Lot #49
   ☑ Faculty (Faculty Office Location: Herman Hall)
   ☐ Student
   ☐ Other

3. If you lost your permit, please explain how it was lost.
   I had my permit in my car when I parked on the morning of Monday, 17 February, at around 7:15 A.M. I went to my office straight afterward and worked all day. After work, I went to a car wash to get my vehicle cleaned. When I finally got home, I realized my permit was missing. I looked all over my car and even called the car wash, but it was nowhere to be found. Most likely, it got lost sometime during the wash.

4. Permit holder declaration
   The information provided above has been filled out completely and truthfully. I acknowledge that if the permit is misplaced or stolen, a renewal fee of $100 must be paid upon issuance of the replacement permit. If the permit is found within a week, I will be reimbursed.

   Authorized signature: Marcus Tiller
   Date: 18 February

5. Only for office use
   Authorized by: Nancy Riddley
   Permit processed on: 18 February
   Parking permit issued:
   ☑ Yes   ☐ No   ☐ Not applicable

153. What is suggested about Mr. Tiller?
(A) He seldom parks his vehicle in Lot #49.
(B) He ate lunch with his coworkers.
(C) He arrived at Herman Hall in the morning.
(D) He is a new university employee.

154. What did NOT happen on February 18?
(A) A document was received by Ms. Riddley.
(B) A penalty was paid.
(C) A parking badge expired.
(D) A parking permit was issued.

Questions 155-157 refer to the following article.

Getting Paid to Travel

9 August – Band Together, a software development firm, is offering an incentive to get employees to go on vacation. Workers will receive $8,000 to travel anywhere they want, on top of their normal vacation pay. —[1]—. This is enough for a family of four to take a trip to Mexico for a week with all expenses paid.

This deal, however, does come with some stipulations. Employees cannot take their office laptops or company phones with them. Also, employees must actually go on a trip—they cannot just relax at home.

—[2]—. This program is based on studies of stress management among office workers. Research has shown that people work harder after returning from vacation because they feel reenergized. Such efficiency leads to higher levels of productivity for a company. —[3]—. The Galvin Institute for Labor Studies has found that less than 50 percent of workers used their vacation days in the last year, with each employee losing four days of productivity due to exhaustion. —[4]—. This program gives a new meaning to the term, "paid vacation."

155. What is the main purpose of the article?

(A) To announce the results of an employment study
(B) To explain a new company initiative
(C) To recommend a travel destination
(D) To describe a new procedure for business expenses

156. What does the article state about having employees go on a vacation?

(A) It helps staff perform better at their jobs.
(B) It makes the workplace more peaceful.
(C) It stops employees from getting sick.
(D) It encourages people to appreciate their families more.

157. In which of the positions marked [1], [2], [3], and [4] does the following sentence best belong?

"It can amount to $5,000 in lost revenue per employee."

(A) [1]
(B) [2]
(C) [3]
(D) [4]

Questions 158-160 refer to the following e-mail.

To	ialonzo@sunshinemail.co.au
From	order@myline.co.au
Date	September 9
Subject	Order #3885

Dear Ms. Alonzo,

Your order (#3885) has been shipped, containing the following items from Myline, Inc.

Quantity	Description	Contents
1	Caribe acrylic paint	24 colors
2	ZTV masking tape	Pack of 2
1	Framed canvas	70x120cm

Unfortunately, the following items are not available at this time:

Quantity	Description	Contents
1	Ubex molding clay	1kg
1	Liysis white paint	1.5 liters

We are sorry for the inconvenience. If you would like to replace these items with similar products that are in stock, you can update your order by visiting your account page at www.myline.co.au. Note that Ubex molding clay is available in half-kilogram packages for AUD12.00, and Manray brand paints, including white, also come in 1.5 liter units. If you make no changes to your order, the original items will be sent when they become available.

You have only been charged for the items that have shipped. When the remainder of your order (or your order for alternative products) is sent, you will be charged accordingly.

We value you as a customer and hope that we can continue to meet your expectations in the future.

Myline Customer Support

158. What is the purpose of the e-mail?

(A) To confirm receipt of a package
(B) To give information about an order
(C) To offer a discount on a product
(D) To provide a change of address

159. What is indicated about the Ubex molding clay?

(A) It is sold in different sizes.
(B) It was paid for by Ms. Alonzo.
(C) It comes in packs of two.
(D) It costs AUD12.00 per kilogram.

160. What is Ms. Alonzo asked to do?

(A) Provide new banking information
(B) Update her customer profile
(C) Send back two defective products
(D) Consider selecting other items

Questions 161-163 refer to the following letter.

International Conservation Weekly
11 Golka Valley
Finglas North
Dublin 8, Ireland 31040

21 August

Alyssa Risseau
4214 W. Bell Dr.
Barcelona, Spain 08039

Dear Ms. Risseau,

Your one-month complimentary subscription to *International Conservation Weekly* ends on 26 August. In order to keep receiving this important information every week, please complete the enclosed subscription renewal form and mail it back by 31 August. Choose from 3, 6, or 12-month subscriptions. Please be aware that our one-year subscription plan is by far the most cost-effective one. In addition, if you choose a six-month or one-year option, you will receive a free tote bag as our gift to you.

We appreciate your support of *International Conservation Weekly* in our ongoing effort to provide you with the most pressing environmental issues from a global perspective. We also request that you give feedback by visiting our Web site at www.internationalconsweekly.org, and completing an online questionnaire.

Sincerely,

Jacob Long
Jacob Long, Subscription Services
Enclosure

161. Why was the letter sent to Ms. Risseau?

(A) To suggest that she re-subscribe
(B) To advertise a new product
(C) To provide a coupon
(D) To ask about an overdue payment

162. For about how long has Ms. Risseau been receiving *International Conservation Weekly*?

(A) For one month
(B) For three months
(C) For six months
(D) For one year

163. What is one thing that Ms. Risseau is asked to do?

(A) Call Mr. Long's colleague
(B) Visit a nature park
(C) Provide her input
(D) Update her contact information

GO ON TO THE NEXT PAGE

Questions 164-167 refer to the following notice.

Changing Hands

Get your sewing needles ready! Sebastian Children's Hospital is organizing a charity event for its Changing Hands initiative that raises money to provide medical supplies to schools in our city. And we want you to help!

Stop by the hospital's front desk anytime in April (the front desk is staffed from 6:00 A.M. to 10:00 P.M.). There, you'll receive a kit with supplies to make a personalized scarf. We have lots of different fabrics to choose from.

Take your knitting materials and make your scarf any way you wish. Get as creative as you like! You are also welcome to stitch your name on it!

Bring it back to us by May 25. Make sure to also include with your business card (see below).

The customized scarves will be available to purchase in June. All the money will go to Changing Hands. Your business card will be posted on the bulletin board by the front entrance.

To find out more, call Sebastian Children's Hospital at (480) 834-9928 or head over to our Web site at www.sebastianhospital.org.

164. What are the readers of the notice asked to do?

(A) To volunteer at a clinic
(B) To distribute medical brochures
(C) To join a charity event
(D) To donate used clothes

165. What is the goal of the Changing Hands program?

(A) To build a new school in the city
(B) To increase a hospital's revenue
(C) To train future doctors
(D) To buy medical supplies for local institutions

166. What is NOT indicated about the personalized scarf?

(A) It can display a name.
(B) It can be made with different fabrics.
(C) It will go on sale in June.
(D) It will be used as a prize.

167. Where will hospital visitors be likely to see the participants' business cards?

(A) In a school's administrative office
(B) Near an entrance
(C) On a Web site
(D) In a community newsletter

Questions 168-171 refer to the following electronic message board.

Group Administrator [8:00 A.M.]
Hey, everyone, we just got the new outfits. If you've already tried yours on, let me know how you like them.

Rick Parsons [8:10 A.M.]
Well, I'm really glad there are no more neckties. Those really got in the way when we were setting the dishes on the tables. They were really troublesome and always got dirty by the end of the dinner shift.

Simone Torres [8:21 A.M.]
Agreed. But the light yellow pants are almost white. And white clothing shows stains from food and coffee. Nobody liked those white uniforms we wore several years back. Does anybody here remember that?

Carl Taranto [8:44 A.M.]
I do like the smart-looking vests and the colorful name tags on the pockets. Good job by whoever designed those!

Rick Parsons [8:49 A.M.]
They're not that light. I don't think stains will be any more visible on these than on what we wear now.

Thomas Contreras [9:07 A.M.]
I like how we're now able to choose between a long-sleeved collared shirt and a short-sleeved shirt. When things are slow, the temperatures in here are pretty comfortable. But when the place gets busy, that can change quickly.

168. Who most likely are the people writing on the message board?

(A) Athletes
(B) Furniture makers
(C) Restaurant servers
(D) Tailors

169. At 8:21 A.M., what does Ms. Torres most likely mean when she writes, "Does anybody here remember that"?

(A) She believes last year's uniforms were better.
(B) She prefers to wear a necktie.
(C) She is worried about the color.
(D) She would like to consider white uniforms.

170. What does Mr. Taranto think about the new outfits?

(A) Their design is outdated.
(B) Their pockets are too large.
(C) They look very stylish.
(D) They need to be brighter.

171. What is Mr. Contreras' opinion about the new uniforms?

(A) He is glad that neckties are optional.
(B) He is glad to have more choices.
(C) He feels that they will get too hot.
(D) He feels that they require alterations.

GO ON TO THE NEXT PAGE

Questions 172-175 refer to the following article.

(JUN 10) – Even for established companies, creating a new brand is a costly, difficult process. For smaller businesses, the challenge is much more difficult. Pruitt McKinnon, founder of The Pen is Mightier than the Sword, initially thought his company's name was clever and memorable. However, as time passed, McKinnon realized that the name stood out too much. —[1]—. "A lot of consumers didn't think the name was appealing," commented McKinnon. "It was unnecessarily long, so I decided to shorten it to 'The Pen is Mightier.'"

Marketing specialist Alyssa Quincy notes that companies have to be careful when changing brand names. "If customers are looking for a certain brand of a product and don't realize a change has been made, they may switch to a different brand," explained Ms. Quincy. "Changes to a logo's design produce similar results." —[2]—.

In spite of the risk, the Marketing Department at The Pen is Mightier pushed ahead with the changes, including major modifications to its logo. Evelyn Vossler-Peters of Wooster Design was hired to create the company's new look. With more than two decades of graphic design experience, Ms. Vossler-Peters has developed a solid reputation for her elegant and modern work, and the ideas she submitted to The Pen is Mightier displays that creativity. —[3]—.

By marketing its new image primarily through social media sites, the company is trying to garner the attention of more Millennials. At the same time, Mr. McKinnon hopes to keep its current customer base happy by maintaining the classic and luxurious feel of the pens. —[4]—. "We hope that our brand remains strong among those that appreciate the care that we put into making our products," he said. "But we also wanted to foster a new generation of loyal customers."

172. What is the purpose of this article?

(A) To publicize a change to a brand name
(B) To review a company's sales figures
(C) To highlight the accomplishments of a marketing specialist
(D) To introduce a new service

173. What does Ms. Quincy warn about?

(A) Introducing additional product features
(B) Changing the appearance of a logo
(C) Expanding business into other regions
(D) Using social media for advertising

174. What is indicated about Ms. Vossler-Peters?

(A) She has designed a new line of pens.
(B) She has worked in her field for a long time.
(C) She graduated from the same school as Mr. McKinnon.
(D) She is a loyal customer of The Pen is Mightier.

175. In which of the positions marked [1], [2], [3], and [4] does the following sentence best belong?

"The department is hoping that the contemporary look will attract a younger group of consumers."

(A) [1]
(B) [2]
(C) [3]
(D) [4]

GO ON TO THE NEXT PAGE

Questions 176-180 refer to the following leaflet and e-mail.

Taupei Optics, Inc.

Taupei Optics, Inc. has been making cameras for more than a century. Built to capture the best, sharpest images possible, these incredible cameras are in high demand and favored by many well-known professional photographers, as well as amateurs, around the world.

Care and Cleaning:
To clean your Taupei camera lens, be sure to use a special brush or blower. Avoid wiping your camera lens with an ordinary cloth as it can scratch or smudge it.

To get the best possible performance, keeping your camera equipment dust-free is of utmost importance. How frequently you will need to clean your device depends on how often you are changing lenses. If you rarely change your lens, the camera only needs cleaning every six months. If you change lenses regularly, clean the camera every three to four weeks. For photographers that change lenses while shooting outdoors, cleaning the camera several times a week is recommended.

Taupei cameras come with a warranty that includes free cleaning services (shipping and handling not included). To prepare your camera for service, remove the lens and place the camera body in a dust-free, sealed plastic bag. Do the same for each of your Taupei lenses. Wrap them in protective packaging and send them to:
Taupei Optics, Inc.
2019 Elizabeth Avenue
Mount Victoria, Wellington 6013

Please ensure that the following is sent inside the parcel: a paper with your contact information including both your home and e-mail address, your phone number, and a check or money order for return shipping. The postage is $25 for a camera with one lens and $5 for each additional lens. If the camera operator has an eyewear prescription, please let us know. Equipment will be returned in between 7 and 14 business days.

Enjoy a lifetime of using your Taupei camera!

To	Taupei Optics, Inc. A/S Department <as.dept@taupeioptics.co.nz>
From	Antonio Cortez <acortez@sandriverphoto.co.nz>
Date	December 4
Subject	Request for update

Hello,

Three weeks ago, I mailed my camera and lenses for cleaning, but I am still waiting for them to be returned. I would like to know when I can expect to receive them back. I sent my camera and three lenses to your Elizabeth Avenue centre on November 14 along with a money order for $25.

Thank you for your time,

Antonio Cortez

176. What is implied about Taupei Optics?

(A) They are guaranteed to operate for a hundred years.
(B) They are custom-made for users that wear glasses.
(C) They are used by famous photographers.
(D) They can only be purchased online.

177. According to the leaflet, what can damage a Taupei camera lens?

(A) Changing it too often
(B) Cleaning it with a liquid
(C) Wiping it with a normal cloth
(D) Placing it in a cabinet

178. What is indicated about camera lenses?

(A) They must be cleaned after every shot.
(B) They require mailing for disposal.
(C) They are very costly to replace.
(D) They affect how often the camera should be cleaned.

179. Why did Mr. Cortez write the e-mail?

(A) To ask about the status of some merchandise
(B) To complain about a damaged package
(C) To confirm that a refund was made
(D) To request a product catalog

180. What did Mr. Cortez fail to do?

(A) Provide the correct amount for a fee
(B) Include a store receipt in a package
(C) Submit his personal information
(D) Indicate the desired delivery time

Questions 181-185 refer to the following brochure and e-mail.

Garden Jose
www.gardenjose.com

Is lawn and garden work taking up too much of your time? Garden Jose can help! We offer our services in locations all over Northern California. Give us a call today for an estimate, and let us take the weight off your shoulders!

Lovely Lawns
Set up a schedule to have one of our teams visit your home daily for routine watering, trimming, and mowing. In just 20 minutes, we can make your lawn look beautiful. We can visit your home early in the morning, during the day while you work, or even in the early evening—it's up to you!

Seasonal Care
Just need a little help from time to time? We're glad to assist! We can visit monthly, quarterly, or just at your convenience, to get your yard looking great for the coming season. In addition to yard work, we offer expert outdoor construction and installation. Whether it's a fountain, a patio, or a new sprinkler system you need, we're the ones for the job.

Pest Control
Uninvited guests such as insects, mice, and harmful varieties of fungus can turn even the most beautiful garden into a nightmare but don't worry. We'll get the pests out and treat your land with our special formula to make sure they don't return.

Custom Resurfacing
We offer a unique, cost-effective alternative to traditional lawns. To see if a resurfaced desert garden could be right for your home, book an appointment with one of our resurfacing specialists for a consultation.

Whatever service you require, you'll only pay once you're completely satisfied—we guarantee it. What are you waiting for? Visit Garden Jose's Web site today and find out about all of our safe, effective, and environmentally-friendly methods for making your lawn and garden the oasis you deserve.

To	info@gardenjose.com
From	nanfang.h@laomeielectronics.com
Subject	Inquiry
Date	May 17

Hello,

I own a home in the suburbs of San Jose. Recently, we have been having a serious problem with ants in our garden, and we are hoping you can assist. Please give me a call at 408-555-1212 to schedule a visit.

Your services come highly recommended by Michelle Ma, a coworker of mine, who lives in Palo Alto. She has been extremely happy with the desert garden that you set up in her front yard.

Best Regards,

Nanfang Hu

181. In the brochure, the word "weight" in paragraph 1, line 2, is closest in meaning to

(A) importance
(B) impact
(C) burden
(D) training

182. What is NOT suggested about Garden Jose?

(A) It tries to protect the environment.
(B) It offers a client guarantee.
(C) It does business in numerous areas.
(D) It provides services for commercial properties.

183. What is mentioned about the Lovely Lawns service?

(A) It requires an on-site consultation.
(B) It requires a safety inspection.
(C) It offers a flexible schedule.
(D) It includes a resurfacing option.

184. Which service will Nanfang Hu most likely request?

(A) Lovely Lawns
(B) Seasonal Care
(C) Pest Control
(D) Custom Resurfacing

185. What is suggested about Palo Alto?

(A) Nanfang Hu lives there.
(B) Garden Jose can send workers there.
(C) It is known for its beautiful gardens.
(D) It is the location of Laomei Electronics' headquarters.

GO ON TO THE NEXT PAGE

Questions 186-190 refer to the following advertisements and e-mail.

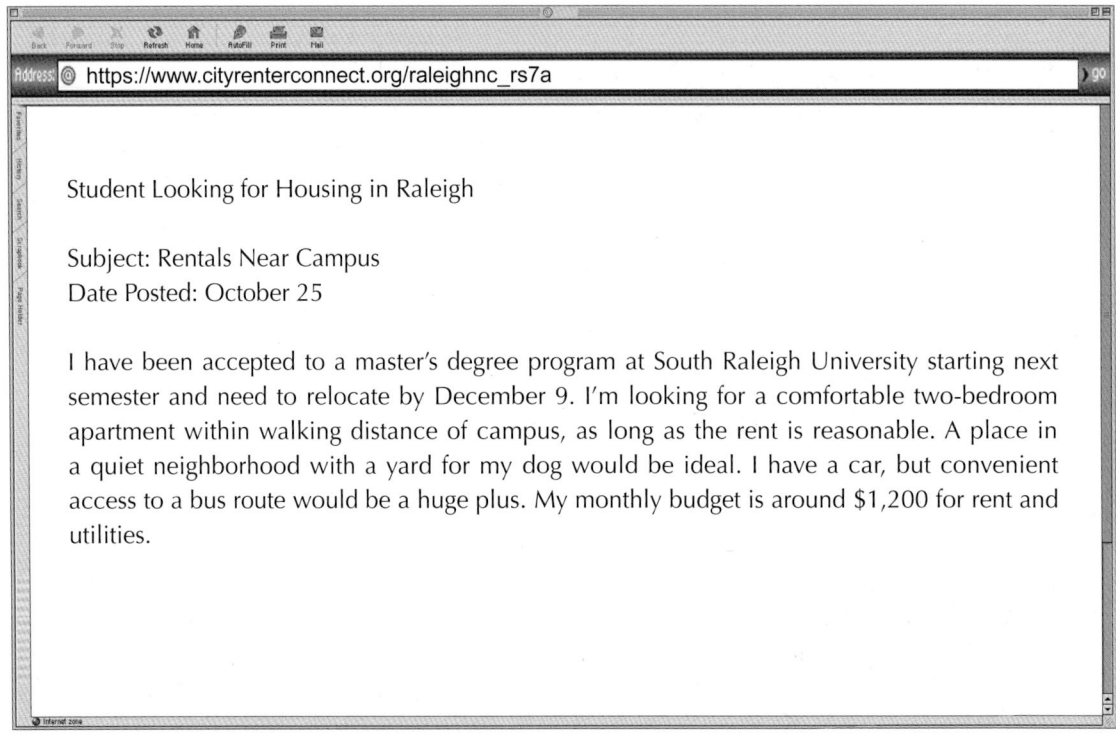

Student Looking for Housing in Raleigh

Subject: Rentals Near Campus
Date Posted: October 25

I have been accepted to a master's degree program at South Raleigh University starting next semester and need to relocate by December 9. I'm looking for a comfortable two-bedroom apartment within walking distance of campus, as long as the rent is reasonable. A place in a quiet neighborhood with a yard for my dog would be ideal. I have a car, but convenient access to a bus route would be a huge plus. My monthly budget is around $1,200 for rent and utilities.

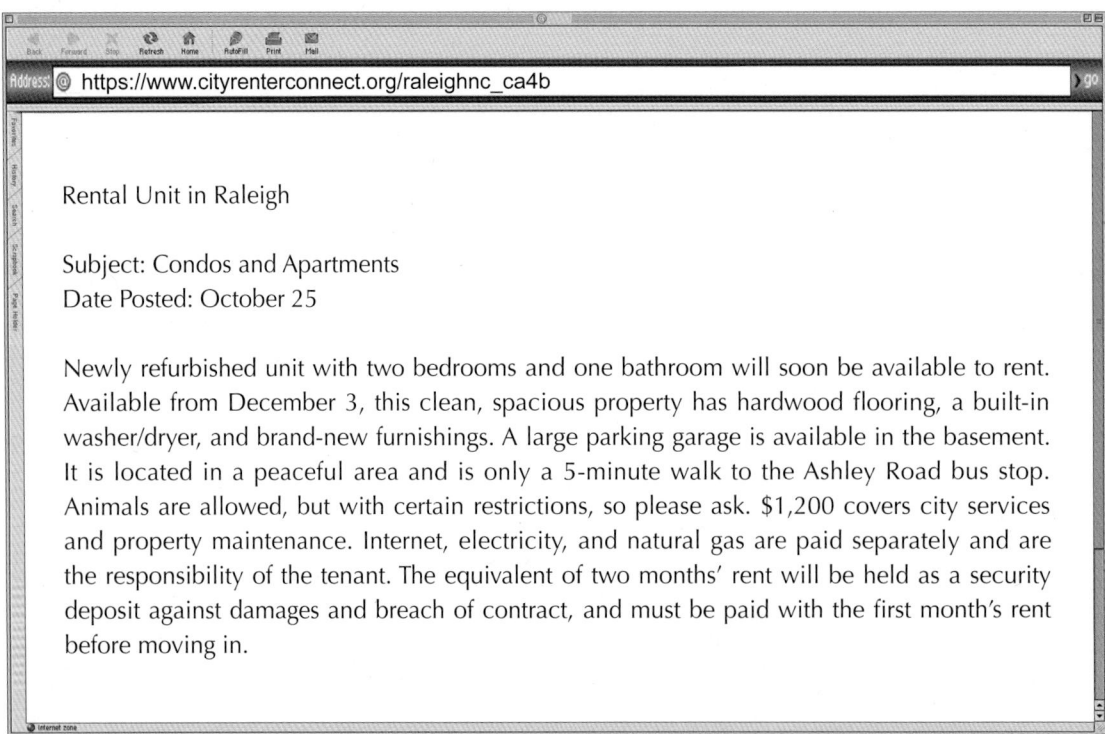

Rental Unit in Raleigh

Subject: Condos and Apartments
Date Posted: October 25

Newly refurbished unit with two bedrooms and one bathroom will soon be available to rent. Available from December 3, this clean, spacious property has hardwood flooring, a built-in washer/dryer, and brand-new furnishings. A large parking garage is available in the basement. It is located in a peaceful area and is only a 5-minute walk to the Ashley Road bus stop. Animals are allowed, but with certain restrictions, so please ask. $1,200 covers city services and property maintenance. Internet, electricity, and natural gas are paid separately and are the responsibility of the tenant. The equivalent of two months' rent will be held as a security deposit against damages and breach of contract, and must be paid with the first month's rent before moving in.

To	Jimmy Merrick <jmerrick@maillink.com>
From	Miranda Santos <miranda_s@salmonpath.com>
Date	October 26
Subject	Condominium

Good afternoon Mr. Merrick,

I recently found your posting on cityrenterconnect.org. Your description sounds like just what I've been trying to find. I would love to take a look at the place sometime this week, if that is okay with you. I'm currently in town taking care of some enrollment paperwork and meeting with faculty. I leave Raleigh on Tuesday, October 30. If the location seems nice, I will plan to move in the first day it's available. I look forward to hearing from you.

Thanks,

Miranda Santos
(919) 555-2577

186. Why is Ms. Santos relocating?

(A) To visit her parents
(B) To begin a teaching position
(C) To live closer to downtown
(D) To attend a new school

187. What aspect of the property does NOT fit Ms. Santos' requirements?

(A) The monthly rent
(B) Parking access
(C) The number of rooms
(D) The proximity to public transit

188. In what situation does Mr. Merrick say that he will require additional information?

(A) When some paperwork is completed
(B) When an appliance breaks
(C) When someone owns a pet
(D) When maintenance is required

189. Why did Ms. Santos send the e-mail?

(A) To revise an online advertisement
(B) To request a property viewing
(C) To ask about some renovations
(D) To negotiate a lease agreement

190. When does Ms. Santos most likely want to begin living in the residence?

(A) On October 26
(B) On October 30
(C) On December 3
(D) On December 9

Questions 191-195 refer to the following e-mails and invoice.

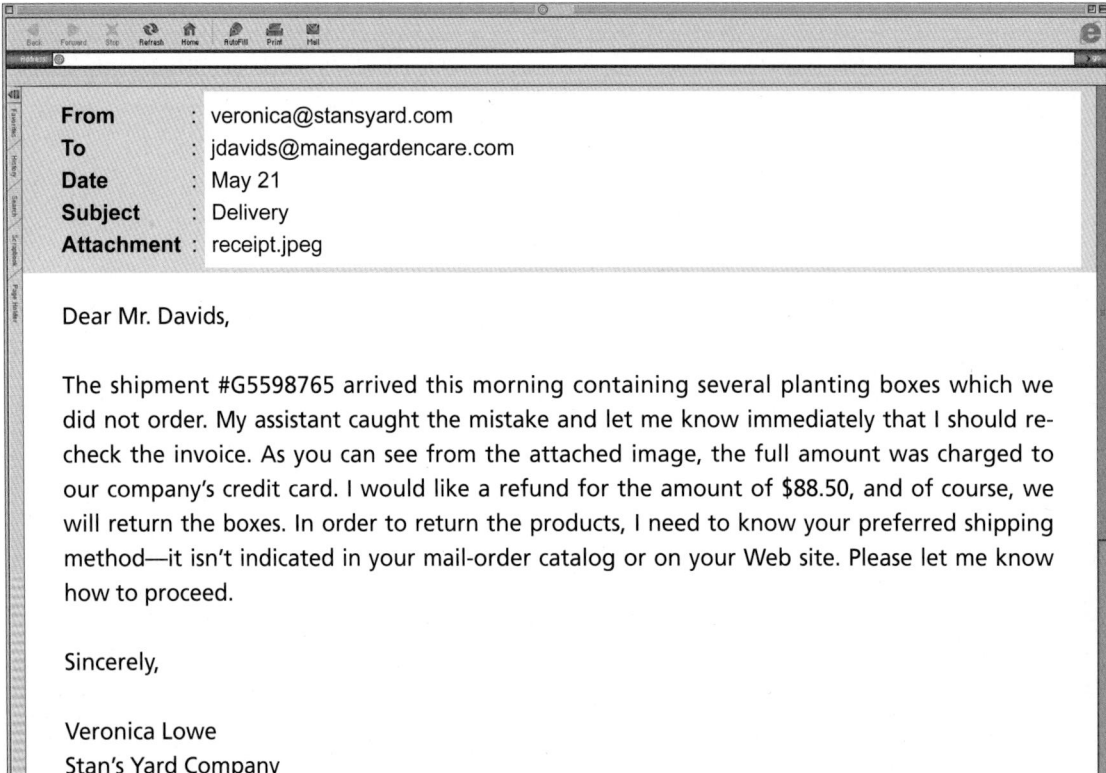

From	: veronica@stansyard.com
To	: jdavids@mainegardencare.com
Date	: May 21
Subject	: Delivery
Attachment	: receipt.jpeg

Dear Mr. Davids,

The shipment #G5598765 arrived this morning containing several planting boxes which we did not order. My assistant caught the mistake and let me know immediately that I should re-check the invoice. As you can see from the attached image, the full amount was charged to our company's credit card. I would like a refund for the amount of $88.50, and of course, we will return the boxes. In order to return the products, I need to know your preferred shipping method—it isn't indicated in your mail-order catalog or on your Web site. Please let me know how to proceed.

Sincerely,

Veronica Lowe
Stan's Yard Company

Invoice

From: Maine Garden Care
2058 Mayflower Ave.
Augusta, ME 04330

To: Stan's Yard Company

ATTN: Veronica Lowe

Order number: #G5598765
Order date: May 13
Charged to: **** **** **** 3321

Description	Product	Quantity	Unit Cost	Total
50kg Verdant fertilizer	VF-250	2	$47.75	$95.50
Maple Planting Box	SKPLW5	3	$29.50	$88.50
5kg Bluegrass seed	Starlawn 408DP	7	$9.25	$64.75
Seed Spreader	Fly 55-A	1	$89.25	$89.25
Total:				$338.00

We value your business.

From	jdavids@mainegardencare.com
To	veronica@stansyard.com
Date	May 21
Subject	Re: Delivery

Thank you for emailing Jeremy Davids at Maine Garden Care. I am on vacation from May 18 through May 29. Please consult the following staff for any questions you may have:

For new accounts and catalog subscriptions: Contact Alice Tyler at atyler@mainegardencare.com

Concerning billing or payment: Contact Justin Hernandez at jhernandez@mainegardencare.com

For order tracking and shipping guidelines: Contact Zach Silva at zsilva@mainegardencare.com

For retail business partnerships: Contact Eileen Bao at ebao@mainegardencare.com

Thank you,

Jeremy Davids
Supervisor, Order Management

191. What information does Ms. Lowe request?

(A) Where to deliver an order
(B) Who to contact for refunds
(C) Why a service fee has been increased
(D) How to send some items

192. In the first e-mail, the word "caught" in paragraph 1, line 2, is closest in meaning to

(A) discovered
(B) captured
(C) received
(D) suffered

193. What product was sent by mistake?

(A) VF-250
(B) SKPLW5
(C) Starlawn 408DP
(D) Fly 55-A

194. Why is Mr. Davids unable to help Ms. Lowe?

(A) He does not handle billing.
(B) He is not in the office.
(C) He is not responsible for deliveries.
(D) He does not have the latest catalog.

195. Whom should Ms. Lowe contact?

(A) Ms. Tyler
(B) Mr. Hernandez
(C) Mr. Silva
(D) Ms. Bao

Questions 196-200 refer to the following article and e-mails.

(SEATTLE) – Tea is currently one of the hottest food and beverage trends. Data from national sales last year shows that tea products brought in an astonishing 25 percent of the $400 billion in food and beverage sales, with this year's forecast to exceed that by as much as 5 percent, according to industry experts.

As is the case with so many food and beverage trends, the recent popularity of tea has its roots in cultural traditions overseas. The sudden surge in local sales is due, in part, to Maria Appleton, founder and CEO of the Café Whole Being franchise. Thirteen years ago, Appleton, then aged 26, accepted a university professorship at Peking University in China, where she found a great variety of tea-related products available in the many local stores. "When I wasn't teaching, I spent all of my time in local tea shops," she said. "I became interested in the health benefits of tea and the culture surrounding it."

After two years in Beijing, Appleton returned to Portland, where she started her localized version of a tea house—a café selling a range of teas in a small rental space. Then, in what seemed like an overnight success, Appleton's teas, like Smoky Hibiscus and Dewdrop Maté, quickly became available, by popular demand, in a chain of stores that opened up from San Diego all the way up to Vancouver, BC. The franchise will be spreading to other locations on the east coast in the near future. Keep your eye on this remarkable entrepreneur and the growth of an amazing café chain.

To	mappleton@cafewholebeing.com
From	dkendall@brightstone.net
Date	July 3
Subject	Congratulations

I've been delighted to see your business getting so much good press lately—congratulations! The lecture that you gave last August was wonderful, and we're hoping that you will consider coming back to share it with this year's new hires. With such a marvelous piece in the *Seattle Observer*, though, I have no doubt that you are getting booked up quickly. Why don't we discuss it over lunch? I'll be free on Tuesday at 10 A.M., Wednesday at 11 A.M., Thursday at 12 P.M., and Friday at 1 P.M. Our old supervisor from Peking University, Richard Lao, may be able to join us, as he will be in town for several days too.

All the best,

Deidre

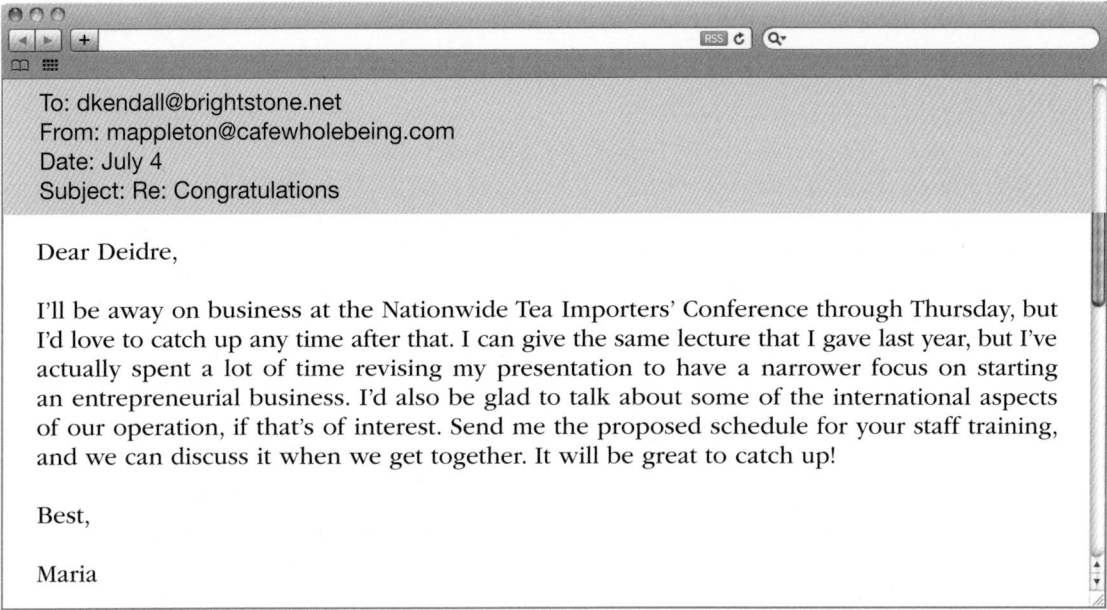

To: dkendall@brightstone.net
From: mappleton@cafewholebeing.com
Date: July 4
Subject: Re: Congratulations

Dear Deidre,

I'll be away on business at the Nationwide Tea Importers' Conference through Thursday, but I'd love to catch up any time after that. I can give the same lecture that I gave last year, but I've actually spent a lot of time revising my presentation to have a narrower focus on starting an entrepreneurial business. I'd also be glad to talk about some of the international aspects of our operation, if that's of interest. Send me the proposed schedule for your staff training, and we can discuss it when we get together. It will be great to catch up!

Best,

Maria

196. What is indicated about the national food and beverage market?

(A) It is the largest industry in Seattle.
(B) It rose by 25 percent in less than one year.
(C) It earns $400 billion in tea sales each year.
(D) It is influenced by products from different countries.

197. What is most likely true about Ms. Appleton and Ms. Kendall?

(A) They are going to a national conference.
(B) They were coworkers in China.
(C) They work as restaurant critics.
(D) They live in Seattle.

198. In the first e-mail, the word "piece" in paragraph 1, line 4, is closest in meaning to

(A) slice
(B) article
(C) fragment
(D) sample

199. When most likely will Ms. Appleton and Ms. Kendall meet?

(A) At 10 A.M.
(B) At 11 A.M.
(C) At 12 P.M.
(D) At 1 P.M.

200. What does Ms. Appleton offer to do?

(A) Schedule a meeting for another day
(B) Provide free drinks for participants
(C) Give advice about hiring additional workers
(D) Speak about founding a new company

Stop! This is the end of the test. If you finish before time is called, you may go back to Part 5, 6, and 7 and check your work.

NO TEST MATERIAL ON THIS PAGE

NO TEST MATERIAL ON THIS PAGE

Answer Keys

MP3, 해석, 해설 온라인 무료 제공
모바일: QR코드 스캔을 통해 MP3 음원 바로 듣기 / 정답, 해석, 해설 바로 보기
PC: 파고다북스 사이트(www.pagodabook.com) 접속 / 로그인 후 다운로드

Listening Comprehension

1 (D)	2 (B)	3 (A)	4 (A)	5 (D)
6 (D)	7 (C)	8 (C)	9 (A)	10 (C)
11 (C)	12 (A)	13 (C)	14 (C)	15 (A)
16 (B)	17 (B)	18 (A)	19 (A)	20 (B)
21 (A)	22 (B)	23 (B)	24 (A)	25 (A)
26 (A)	27 (B)	28 (C)	29 (B)	30 (A)
31 (B)	32 (C)	33 (A)	34 (D)	35 (C)
36 (D)	37 (A)	38 (D)	39 (B)	40 (B)
41 (A)	42 (C)	43 (A)	44 (B)	45 (A)
46 (D)	47 (B)	48 (A)	49 (D)	50 (D)
51 (D)	52 (B)	53 (A)	54 (B)	55 (A)
56 (B)	57 (D)	58 (A)	59 (D)	60 (A)
61 (A)	62 (C)	63 (D)	64 (A)	65 (D)
66 (A)	67 (C)	68 (C)	69 (A)	70 (B)
71 (C)	72 (C)	73 (D)	74 (B)	75 (C)
76 (B)	77 (D)	78 (C)	79 (B)	80 (B)
81 (C)	82 (B)	83 (C)	84 (A)	85 (C)
86 (A)	87 (D)	88 (B)	89 (A)	90 (B)
91 (B)	92 (A)	93 (D)	94 (C)	95 (A)
96 (D)	97 (B)	98 (C)	99 (D)	100 (B)

Reading Comprehension

101 (B)	102 (A)	103 (C)	104 (C)	105 (B)
106 (D)	107 (D)	108 (A)	109 (A)	110 (C)
111 (D)	112 (C)	113 (C)	114 (B)	115 (C)
116 (C)	117 (C)	118 (B)	119 (A)	120 (A)
121 (A)	122 (A)	123 (C)	124 (C)	125 (A)
126 (C)	127 (B)	128 (B)	129 (B)	130 (A)
131 (D)	132 (B)	133 (A)	134 (C)	135 (B)
136 (C)	137 (A)	138 (C)	139 (A)	140 (B)
141 (D)	142 (C)	143 (D)	144 (A)	145 (D)
146 (C)	147 (B)	148 (C)	149 (C)	150 (D)
151 (C)	152 (D)	153 (C)	154 (C)	155 (B)
156 (A)	157 (D)	158 (B)	159 (A)	160 (D)
161 (A)	162 (A)	163 (C)	164 (C)	165 (D)
166 (D)	167 (B)	168 (C)	169 (C)	170 (C)
171 (B)	172 (A)	173 (B)	174 (B)	175 (C)
176 (C)	177 (C)	178 (D)	179 (A)	180 (A)
181 (C)	182 (D)	183 (C)	184 (C)	185 (B)
186 (D)	187 (A)	188 (C)	189 (B)	190 (C)
191 (D)	192 (A)	193 (B)	194 (B)	195 (C)
196 (D)	197 (B)	198 (B)	199 (D)	200 (D)

초판 1쇄 인쇄 2018년 7월 4일
초판 1쇄 발행 2018년 7월 4일
초판 11쇄 발행 2024년 9월 30일

지 은 이 | 파고다교육그룹 언어교육연구소
펴 낸 이 | 박경실
펴 낸 곳 | **PAGODA Books** 파고다북스
출판등록 | 2005년 5월 27일 제 300-2005-90호
주　　소 | 06614 서울특별시 서초구 강남대로 419, 19층(서초동, 파고다타워)
전　　화 | (02) 6940-4070
팩　　스 | (02) 536-0660
홈페이지 | www.pagodabook.com

저작권자 | ⓒ 2018 파고다아카데미

이 책의 저작권은 저자와 출판사에 있습니다. 서면에 의한 저작권자와 출판사의 허락 없이
내용의 일부 혹은 전부를 인용 및 복제하거나 발췌하는 것을 금합니다.

Copyright ⓒ 2018 by PAGODA Academy

All rights reserved. No part of this publication may be reproduced, stored
in a retrieval system, or transmitted, in any form, or by any means, electronic,
mechanical, photocopying, recording or otherwise, without the prior written
permission of the copyright holder and the publisher.

ISBN 978-89-6281-817-8 (13740)

파고다북스　　www.pagodabook.com
파고다 어학원　www.pagoda21.com
파고다 인강　　www.pagodastar.com
테스트 클리닉　www.testclinic.com

▎낙장 및 파본은 구매처에서 교환해 드립니다.

PAGODA Books

파고다토익 시험 직전 마무리 모의고사 Vol. 2

TEST 2

해설 바로 보기

음원 바로 듣기

PAGODA Books

시험 진행 안내

❶ 시험 시간: 120분(2시간)
  · Listening Comprehension 100문제: 45분
  · Reading Comprehension 100문제: 75분
  · L/C 진행 후 휴식 시간 없이 바로 R/C 진행

❷ 준비물
  · 컴퓨터용 사인펜 또는 연필

❸ 시험 응시 준수 사항
  · 시험 시작 10분 전 입실 (이후에는 입실 불가)
  · 종료 30분 전과 10분 전에 시험 종료 공지함
  · 휴대전화의 전원을 꺼둘 것

❹ OMR 답안지 표기 요령
  · 반드시 컴퓨터용 사인펜 또는 연필로 표기
  · 개인정보, 문제번호, 단체명, 문제번호, 학과(부서) 및 학번코드 표기
    (학과(부서)코드는 별도 공지)

※ 개인정보, 문제번호, 학과(부서)코드를 틀리게 표기했을 경우 채점 및 성적 확인이 불가능하므로 주의하시기 바랍니다.

답안 작성 요령 Sample

○	●	Ⓑ	Ⓒ	Ⓓ
×	Ⓐ	Ⓑ	⊗	Ⓓ
×	Ⓐ	Ⓑ	Ⓒ︎	Ⓓ
×	Ⓐ	Ⓑ	Ⓒ	Ⓓ
×	Ⓐ	Ⓑ̸	Ⓒ	Ⓓ

LISTENING TEST

In the Listening test, you will be asked to demonstrate how well you understand spoken English. The entire listening test will last approximately 45 minutes. There are four parts, and directions are given for each part. You must mark your answers on the separate answer sheet. Do not write your answers in your test book.

PART 1

Directions: For each question in this part, you will hear four statements about a picture in your test book. When you hear the statements, you must select the one statement that best describes what you see in the picture. Then find the number of the question on your answer sheet and mark your answer. The statements will not be printed in your test book and will be spoken only one time.

Statement (B), "A man is pointing at a document," is the best description of the picture, so you should select answer (B) and mark it on your answer sheet.

1.

2.

GO ON TO THE NEXT PAGE

3.

4.

5.

6.

PART 2

Directions: You will hear a question or statement and three responses spoken in English. They will not be printed in your test book and will be spoken only one time. Select the best response to the question or statement and mark the letter (A), (B), or (C) on your answer sheet.

7. Mark your answer on your answer sheet.
8. Mark your answer on your answer sheet.
9. Mark your answer on your answer sheet.
10. Mark your answer on your answer sheet.
11. Mark your answer on your answer sheet.
12. Mark your answer on your answer sheet.
13. Mark your answer on your answer sheet.
14. Mark your answer on your answer sheet.
15. Mark your answer on your answer sheet.
16. Mark your answer on your answer sheet.
17. Mark your answer on your answer sheet.
18. Mark your answer on your answer sheet.
19. Mark your answer on your answer sheet.
20. Mark your answer on your answer sheet.
21. Mark your answer on your answer sheet.
22. Mark your answer on your answer sheet.
23. Mark your answer on your answer sheet.
24. Mark your answer on your answer sheet.
25. Mark your answer on your answer sheet.
26. Mark your answer on your answer sheet.
27. Mark your answer on your answer sheet.
28. Mark your answer on your answer sheet.
29. Mark your answer on your answer sheet.
30. Mark your answer on your answer sheet.
31. Mark your answer on your answer sheet.

PART 3

Directions: You will hear some conversations between two or more people. You will be asked to answer three questions about what the speakers say in each conversation. Select the best response to each question and mark the letter (A), (B), (C), or (D) on your answer sheet. The conversations will not be printed in your test book and will be spoken only one time.

32. What problem does the man mention?
    (A) A coupon is no longer valid.
    (B) His lunch did not taste good.
    (C) His credit card is at home.
    (D) A receipt is wrong.

33. What does the man say he wants to do?
    (A) Receive information about holding an event
    (B) Negotiate some pricing
    (C) Participate in a customer survey
    (D) Talk to the head chef about his recent experience

34. Why is the man asked to wait?
    (A) Some tables are being arranged.
    (B) An employee is busy.
    (C) Some dishes take a while to prepare.
    (D) A payment is being processed.

35. Where does the woman most likely work?
    (A) At a grocery store
    (B) At a manufacturing plant
    (C) At a shipping company
    (D) At an appliance retailer

36. What is the man asking about?
    (A) The results of a test
    (B) The quantity of an item
    (C) The estimated delivery date
    (D) The production cost

37. What does the woman recommend?
    (A) Contacting another vendor
    (B) Adjusting a schedule
    (C) Reading customer testimonials
    (D) Limiting size options

38. Where do the women most likely work?
    (A) At a hotel
    (B) At a restaurant
    (C) At a car rental agency
    (D) At an airline company

39. What is the man disappointed about?
    (A) A travel alert
    (B) A damaged package
    (C) An additional fee
    (D) A delayed trip

40. What information will the man be asked to provide?
    (A) The dates of some reservations
    (B) A photo ID
    (C) A credit card number
    (D) The mailing address of a company

41. Where most likely are the speakers?
    (A) At a gym
    (B) At a computer shop
    (C) At a university
    (D) At a dental office

42. According to the man, why should Ms. Yoko set up an account?
    (A) To make a reservation
    (B) To provide some comments
    (C) To watch a video
    (D) To use a payment service

43. What does Candice give to Ms. Yoko?
    (A) A registration form
    (B) A set of directions
    (C) A list of prices
    (D) A coupon

GO ON TO THE NEXT PAGE

44. Where does the conversation most likely take place?

(A) At a sales event
(B) At an awards ceremony
(C) At an industry convention
(D) At a retirement dinner

45. What does the man's company develop?

(A) Digital cameras
(B) Software programs
(C) Computer monitors
(D) Speaker systems

46. How does the man prefer to be contacted?

(A) By fax
(B) By e-mail
(C) By social media
(D) By phone

47. Why has the man contacted the woman?

(A) To announce an increase in his company's prices
(B) To inform her about a delay
(C) To alert her about an upcoming promotion
(D) To negotiate the terms of a contract

48. What information does the woman share?

(A) A schedule is not easy to coordinate.
(B) A payment has been submitted.
(C) An employee will not arrive on time.
(D) A product will be returned soon.

49. What does the man say about Barrel Photos?

(A) It has flexible hours.
(B) Its fees are affordable.
(C) Its location is convenient.
(D) It employs experienced staff.

50. What is the man doing on Thursday?

(A) Passing out a questionnaire
(B) Transferring to a different team
(C) Attending a recruitment event
(D) Holding a seminar

51. Why does the man say, "you're the top performing salesperson at our company"?

(A) To provide a reason for a request
(B) To congratulate a coworker on a sale
(C) To express confidence about a project
(D) To inform a colleague of a revised process

52. What does the woman need to do on Thursday?

(A) Visit another branch
(B) Meet with some executives
(C) Host a corporate dinner
(D) Finish an assignment

53. What did the woman recently do?

(A) She started a business.
(B) She wrote a book.
(C) She contributed some tools.
(D) She received a prize.

54. What is the woman looking forward to?

(A) A television show
(B) A newspaper article
(C) A guest appearance
(D) A large donation

55. Why does the woman say, "we have a class at 7 P.M. tomorrow"?

(A) To offer an invitation
(B) To recommend a product
(C) To make an apology
(D) To request feedback

56. Why is the man contacting the woman?

(A) To open an account
(B) To inquire about an invoice
(C) To check on a reservation
(D) To extend a subscription

57. What did the man do in April?

(A) He visited another country.
(B) He started a new job.
(C) He bought a device.
(D) He registered for a program.

58. According to the woman, what was the man told to do?

(A) Speak with a manager
(B) Make a deposit
(C) Submit a document
(D) Turn off an option

---

59. Who most likely is the man?

(A) An engineer
(B) A store manager
(C) A reporter
(D) A computer repairperson

60. What is the topic of the conversation?

(A) A product launch
(B) Results of a customer survey
(C) The expansion of a shop
(D) A price increase

61. According to the woman, what will most likely happen in September?

(A) Merchandise will be available for sale.
(B) A story will be released.
(C) A television commercial will be broadcast.
(D) Discount coupons will be distributed.

National Entertainment May Pop Chart		
	Name	**Artist**
#1	*Autumn Winds*	Kelly Harkson
#2	*One More Time*	Stacey Jones
#3	*Together Forever*	Raya Summers
#4	*Graceful Surrender*	Lisa Twain

62. Where do the speakers most likely work?

(A) At a music store
(B) At a concert hall
(C) At a recording studio
(D) At a talent agency

63. Look at the graphic. Who does the woman want to invite for an event?

(A) Kelly Harkson
(B) Stacey Jones
(C) Raya Summers
(D) Lisa Twain

64. What does the man instruct the woman to do?

(A) Analyze some data
(B) Obtain some contact information
(C) Clean a storage room
(D) Hire a consultant

GO ON TO THE NEXT PAGE

Zepplin Music Festival
July 13-16
Lakehurst Fairgrounds
Tickets $35

(A) GUESTS HAVE TO CHECK IN AT SECURITY BOOTH

(B) DO NOT BLOCK ENTRANCE

(C) SLOWLY APPROACH ENTRANCE

(D) THIS PARKING LOT IS UNDER VIDEO SURVEILLANCE

65. What project will the speakers be working on?

(A) Organizing a hotel opening
(B) Updating a Web site
(C) Producing an album
(D) Developing a program

66. Look at the graphic. Which date will the man most likely attend the festival?

(A) July 13
(B) July 14
(C) July 15
(D) July 16

67. Who is Shayna Lane?

(A) A musical artist
(B) A studio executive
(C) An event planner
(D) A newspaper reporter

68. Look at the graphic. Which sign does the woman refer to?

(A) Sign A
(B) Sign B
(C) Sign C
(D) Sign D

69. Why is the woman at the warehouse?

(A) To participate in a job interview
(B) To deliver some machines
(C) To perform an inspection
(D) To lead a training session

70. What does the man give to the woman?

(A) A parking pass
(B) A building directory
(C) A receipt
(D) A schedule

PART 4

Directions: You will hear some talks given by a single speaker. You will be asked to answer three questions about what the speaker says in each talk. Select the best response to each question and mark the letter (A), (B), (C), or (D) on your answer sheet. The talks will not be printed in your test book and will be spoken only one time.

71. What products does the company sell?

    (A) Work uniforms
    (B) Kitchen appliances
    (C) Computer accessories
    (D) Storage shelves

72. What does the speaker emphasize about the products?

    (A) A wide range of models are available.
    (B) Customers have given positive reviews.
    (C) They are affordable.
    (D) They are easy to carry.

73. What is being offered at a discount for this month?

    (A) Shipping
    (B) Installation
    (C) An extended warranty
    (D) On-site consultations

74. What will Ms. Fowler do next month?

    (A) Give a presentation
    (B) Transfer to a new office
    (C) Participate in a board meeting
    (D) Attend a regional conference

75. What company policy does the speaker mention?

    (A) Providing frequent evaluations
    (B) Offering training sessions
    (C) Issuing quarterly bonuses
    (D) Finding qualified candidates internally

76. Why should the listeners talk to Mr. Kim?

    (A) To learn more about a position
    (B) To receive a letter of recommendation
    (C) To review a new office procedure
    (D) To discuss their remaining vacation days

77. What is the subject of today's show?

    (A) Acquiring funding
    (B) Expanding product lines
    (C) Increasing work efficiency
    (D) Obtaining a business license

78. According to the speaker, what did Mr. Rhee recently do?

    (A) Lead a workshop
    (B) Redesign a Web site
    (C) Write a book
    (D) Conduct a survey

79. What are listeners encouraged to do?

    (A) Sign up for a marketing course
    (B) Attend a convention
    (C) Visit a local store
    (D) Talk about their experiences

80. What product does the speaker's company make?

    (A) Air conditioners
    (B) Kitchen supplies
    (C) Packaging boxes
    (D) Computer accessories

81. What is the speaker calling about?

    (A) A suggestion for a presentation
    (B) An advertisement for a product
    (C) A timetable for a conference
    (D) An issue with an image

82. What does the speaker request?

    (A) Free installation
    (B) A discount
    (C) Some photos
    (D) A rush delivery

GO ON TO THE NEXT PAGE

13

83. Who most likely are the listeners?

    (A) Broadcasting executives
    (B) Marketing specialists
    (C) News reporters
    (D) Personal trainers

84. What is the purpose of the talk?

    (A) To describe a seminar schedule
    (B) To discuss a contest
    (C) To introduce a new product
    (D) To explain a new ad campaign

85. What does the speaker imply when he says, "There's a break room with vending machines just around the corner"?

    (A) The listeners had the wrong directions to the vending machines.
    (B) The listeners may purchase snacks from the vending machines.
    (C) The listeners will gather at the vending machines soon.
    (D) The listeners should avoid damaging the vending machines.

86. Where does the speaker most likely work?

    (A) At a restaurant
    (B) At a hospital
    (C) At an airport
    (D) At a library

87. What does the speaker mean when he says, "Your satisfaction is our top priority"?

    (A) He is dissatisfied with a vendor.
    (B) He is thinking about revising a business policy.
    (C) He is asking for feedback about a service.
    (D) He is making an effort to resolve an issue.

88. What does the speaker ask the listener to do?

    (A) Return a phone call
    (B) Review a bill
    (C) Update a system
    (D) Check a Web site

89. What is the purpose of the event?

    (A) To honor a company executive
    (B) To celebrate a branch opening
    (C) To praise a team's success
    (D) To welcome a new manager

90. According to the speaker, what did Howard Dominguez do?

    (A) He helped acquire many major client accounts.
    (B) He increased a company's international presence.
    (C) He made an award-winning product.
    (D) He started a training program.

91. What most likely will happen next?

    (A) Pamphlets will be distributed.
    (B) Food will be served.
    (C) A present will be given.
    (D) A film will be shown.

92. In what department does the speaker most likely work?

    (A) Sales
    (B) Advertising
    (C) Personnel
    (D) Accounting

93. What does the speaker mean when he says, "we've got over 40 applications so far"?

    (A) Some résumés are incomplete.
    (B) Several applicants have been contacted already.
    (C) A submission deadline would be extended.
    (D) A job posting was successful.

94. What does the speaker ask Wally to do?

    (A) Schedule some interviews
    (B) Review an office floor plan
    (C) Have more work areas set up
    (D) Check on the status of an order

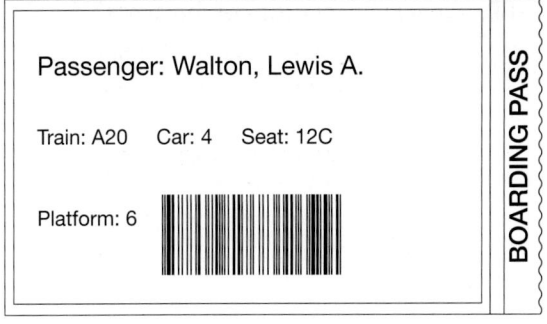
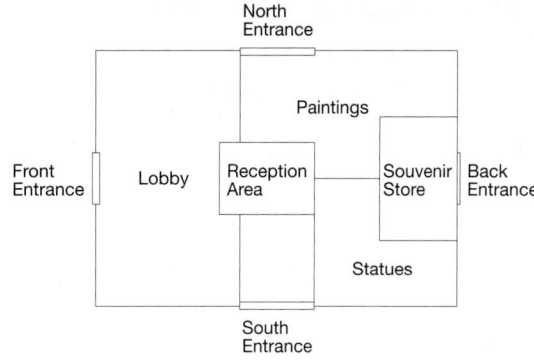

95. What is the announcement about?

(A) A missing item
(B) A platform change
(C) A late train
(D) A canceled departure

96. Look at the graphic. Which code should Lewis Walton pay attention to now?

(A) A20
(B) 4
(C) 12C
(D) 6

97. What will be announced later?

(A) How to upgrade seats
(B) Where to retrieve baggage
(C) When maintenance will be completed
(D) Whom to talk to for a refund

98. What is the purpose of the meeting?

(A) To share ideas for a gallery pamphlet
(B) To discuss qualifications of a tour guide
(C) To get ready for an exhibition opening
(D) To describe features of a new art course

99. Look at the graphic. Which entrance will visitors use on Saturday?

(A) The front entrance
(B) The back entrance
(C) The north entrance
(D) The south entrance

100. What does the speaker say will happen in the reception area?

(A) Snacks will be provided.
(B) An art auction will be held.
(C) A live concert will take place.
(D) Famous artists will give autographs.

This is the end of the Listening test. Turn to Part 5 in your test book.

GO ON TO THE NEXT PAGE

READING TEST

In the Reading test, you will read a variety of texts and answer several different types of reading comprehension questions. The entire Reading test will last 75 minutes. There are three parts, and directions are given for each part. You are encouraged to answer as many questions as possible within the time allowed.

You must mark your answers on the separate answer sheet. Do not write your answers in your test book.

PART 5

Directions: A word or phrase is missing in each of the sentences below. Four answer choices are given below each sentence. Select the best answer to complete the sentence. Then mark the letter (A), (B), (C), or (D) on your answer sheet.

101. Mr. Granger is going to operate a booth at the expo with ------- design team.

    (A) his
    (B) he
    (C) him
    (D) himself

102. Although her books are educational, Ms. Tuscano feels readers will ------- be entertained.

    (A) most
    (B) almost
    (C) still
    (D) enough

103. ------- from Monday's departmental workshop have been emailed to all of the managers who were unable to participate.

    (A) Breaks
    (B) Speakers
    (C) Notes
    (D) Offices

104. All department managers will have a meeting with the HR director -------- interviewing the job candidates.

    (A) as if
    (B) although
    (C) frequent
    (D) before

105. Since rain is ------- on Sunday, the Camdera City biannual marathon fundraiser was rescheduled to November 12.

    (A) liked
    (B) likely
    (C) likelihood
    (D) likeable

106. The new backpacking tent designed by Nugear can withstand extreme punishment, even ------- the harshest storms.

    (A) from
    (B) next
    (C) down
    (D) onto

107. Ms. Grenier will be temporarily working in Chicago so that she can ------- on the new branch.

    (A) to concentrate
    (B) concentrates
    (C) concentrate
    (D) concentrating

108. It is ------- that the manager be made aware of any customer complaints when they occur.

    (A) rapid
    (B) hectic
    (C) valid
    (D) critical

109. PYU Auto executives met this afternoon to discuss ------- to accelerate the production of NX-579 engines.

(A) how
(B) test
(C) for
(D) later

110. According to the ------- of this agreement, the trial version of the TZ software may not be used for commercial purposes.

(A) terms
(B) practices
(C) remarks
(D) signs

111. For the chemicals to mix and react properly, the temperature must remain ------- the same throughout the process.

(A) exactly
(B) exactness
(C) exacted
(D) exact

112. The Highway 50 expansion project has been authorized ------- concerns about its impact on the environment.

(A) after
(B) except
(C) within
(D) despite

113. There are several software programs at our store that will help ------- to learn computer skills.

(A) yourself
(B) you
(C) yourselves
(D) your

114. The sponsor of the National Art Contest limits ------- to one per person.

(A) members
(B) entries
(C) conditions
(D) directions

115. The second Monday of every month is ------- the regional manager meeting is held.

(A) why
(B) when
(C) since
(D) yet

116. Now that Harpo Furnishings has opened an online store, customers can browse items a week ------- their arrival in shops.

(A) among
(B) ahead of
(C) by
(D) away from

117. The Transit Authority is seeking a subway train ------- with a minimum of three years of experience.

(A) operator
(B) operational
(C) operation
(D) operating

118. Remember to update the list of ------- qualifications so that only those who are suitable for the position will apply.

(A) equivalent
(B) essential
(C) obliged
(D) potential

119. The bill for the suite was ------- expected because the hotel waived the room service charges.

(A) less than
(B) considering that
(C) much more
(D) slightly less

120. For $40, patrons can have a customized message ------- on any trophy or plaque.

(A) shined
(B) developed
(C) enrolled
(D) engraved

GO ON TO THE NEXT PAGE

121. Due to the rainy weather, Renault Amusement Park will probably get ------- visitors during the weekend.

    (A) fewer
    (B) greater
    (C) each
    (D) either

122. Since the rates at the Dundale Hotel have gone up, Ramble Electronics will have its annual conference ------- this year.

    (A) quite
    (B) elsewhere
    (C) lately
    (D) rarely

123. The quarterly conference will focus on the environmental issues ------- the fishing communities of Greenland.

    (A) face
    (B) are facing
    (C) have faced
    (D) facing

124. Brandon Wu was nominated as Representative of the Year ------- his ongoing commitment to excellent customer service.

    (A) for
    (B) about
    (C) since
    (D) while

125. AGZ Bank ------- a comprehensive online banking system to make paying bills and transferring money more convenient.

    (A) to be introduced
    (B) has introduced
    (C) introducing
    (D) is introduced

126. ------- some stores will no longer carry our products next year, other new stores have shown interest.

    (A) Even though
    (B) In spite of
    (C) Furthermore
    (D) On the other hand

127. The e-mail sent by the CEO stated that employees may order ------- they like at the company dinner.

    (A) if
    (B) most
    (C) those
    (D) whatever

128. Returning clients at Al's Furniture Store ------- get a half-price discount on their tenth purchase.

    (A) convincingly
    (B) concisely
    (C) customarily
    (D) completely

129. Mr. Lee decided to work ------- with Prager Associates regarding any legal issues.

    (A) exclusive
    (B) excluded
    (C) exclusively
    (D) excluding

130. The seasonal sales event will be held on a date that ------- the opening of an outlet store.

    (A) converts to
    (B) replies to
    (C) coincides with
    (D) complies with

PART 6

Directions: Read the texts that follow. A word, phrase, or sentence is missing in parts of each text. Four answer choices for each question are given below the text. Select the best answer to complete the text. Then mark the letter (A), (B), (C), or (D) on your answer sheet.

Questions 131-134 refer to the following e-mail.

To: David O'Rourke <dorourke@lastline.co.ca>
From: Elizabeth Dewey <lizd@hazmedia.com>
Date: July 22
Subject: Incentive system

Hi David,

It was great meeting you recently in Newark. During our conversation, you mentioned the employee incentive system you introduced last year. You stated that the system ------- a competition tracking production time, with bonuses for the departments with the fewest
131.
delays. I was impressed by how this system increased ------- and profitability. This seems
132.
------- the most effective way to let the staff know how much we value their hard work and
133.
dedication. -------. Would you be willing to discuss with me how you tracked the production
134.
time and calculated the bonus amounts?

I hope to speak with you soon.

Sincerely,

Elizabeth Dewey

131. (A) featuring
 (B) featured
 (C) will feature
 (D) to feature

132. (A) efficiency
 (B) costs
 (C) choice
 (D) requirement

133. (A) contrary to
 (B) around
 (C) like
 (D) as if

134. (A) I was surprised to hear about your results.
 (B) We are proud of our employees' accomplishments.
 (C) I assure you this will not happen in the future.
 (D) I wish to implement a similar program at my company.

GO ON TO THE NEXT PAGE

19

Questions 135-138 refer to the following memo.

From: Gordon Caulman
To: All employees
Subject: Update
Date: 20 March

Dear all,

I want to thank everyone for their hard work so far this year. As you may be aware, Caulman Furniture will be ------- its third store in the summer. The additional retail location will be situated right across the street from Hammock Mall on Shorelake Boulevard.
135.

Management will be taking applications for sales clerks and inventory control specialists ------- 31 May. We will interview the successful candidates from 1 June to 5 June, and ------- is set to start five days later. -------.
136. **137.** **138.**

Sincerely,

Gordon Caulman
President of Caulman Furniture

135. (A) remodeling
(B) opening
(C) relocating
(D) expanding

136. (A) over
(B) by
(C) until
(D) within

137. (A) train
(B) trains
(C) trained
(D) training

138. (A) Please call Caulman Furniture's hotline if you have not received a reply.
(B) The front entrance will not be accessible during the construction work.
(C) All of the necessary paperwork will be included in the packet.
(D) Make sure to let your friends know about this opportunity.

Questions 139-142 refer to the following letter.

PGD Financial Services
964 Harbor Blvd
Weehawken, NJ 07086

December 20

Daniel Marquez
25 Newark Street
Hoboken, NJ 07030

Dear Mr. Marquez,

On December 16, as you asked, our staff investigated your transfer of $786.44 completed via our online banking system on December 13. This transaction was accidentally processed twice, and the same amount was sent again the following day. -------, on December 17, we made the necessary adjustment. On that day, we ------- $786.44 back to your account. We have updated your online statement ------- the cancellation of the second transfer. -------. If you have further questions about this matter, please feel free to call me at 1-800-555-1212, extension 254.

Best wishes,

Robert McCullock
PGD Financial Services Transaction Reconciliation Dept.

139. (A) As a result
(B) Furthermore
(C) On the other hand
(D) To be exact

140. (A) will credit
(B) credits
(C) are crediting
(D) credited

141. (A) that reflect on
(B) to reflect
(C) reflecting in
(D) a reflection of

142. (A) I apologize for any worry or inconvenience this situation may have caused you.
(B) I would like to tell you about several investments I think may be of interest.
(C) Statements can also be sent to your home or office.
(D) A new representative will be assigned to this account.

GO ON TO THE NEXT PAGE

Questions 143-146 refer to the following notice.

As discussed in this month's employee meeting, management here at Palm Desert Mutual has approved a project to make an area for its employees' ------- in the lot directly behind the building.
143.

The field to the west of the recycling area will be paved, painted, and furnished with several hundred parking spaces. ------- will be equipped with a sensor and can accommodate even large trucks. Construction should take ------- five days to finish.
144. .... **145.**

If you would like to park in one of these spaces, please add your name to the list in the operations managers' office. -------. Palm Desert Mutual cannot guarantee that every employee will get a spot.
146.

143. (A) furniture
(B) vehicles
(C) waste
(D) shipments

144. (A) Every
(B) Each
(C) Anything
(D) None

145. (A) rough
(B) rougher
(C) roughly
(D) roughness

146. (A) You may be asked to assist with the construction.
(B) All paperwork must be stored according to company regulations.
(C) Employees are reminded to keep their personal belongings with them at all times.
(D) Spaces will be provided on a first-come, first-served basis.

PART 7

Directions: In this part you will read a selection of texts, such as magazine and newspaper articles, e-mails, and instant messages. Each text or set of texts is followed by several questions. Select the best answer for each question and mark the letter (A), (B), (C), or (D) on your answer sheet.

Questions 147-148 refer to the following form.

Mark it Up: 21st Century Design
June 21 – June 22
3460 E. Coast Road
Point Area, CA 95468

Name: Howard Moss
Title: Art Director
Company: Birdpond Studios
Address: 1028 E. Wildwood Ave., Daly City, CA 94015
E-mail: hmoss@birdponds.com
Phone: 650-555-4337

I will participate on:
☐ June 21: All-day session, including the keynote presentation, tutorial classes, buffet brunch, and networking opportunities
(9:30 A.M. – 7 P.M.)
☑ June 22: Half-day session, including a general issues discussion forum, lectures by industry leaders, and closing remarks
(9:30 A.M. – 1 P.M.)

Fee:
☑ One day ($175)
☐ Two days ($300)

---

147. What is the purpose of the form?

(A) To sign up for a conference
(B) To organize a lecture
(C) To request a different venue
(D) To ask for a payment

148. According to the form, what will Mr. Moss most likely do?

(A) Give an opening speech
(B) Eat a provided meal
(C) Apply for a discount
(D) Engage in conversations

GO ON TO THE NEXT PAGE

Questions 149-150 refer to the following e-mail.

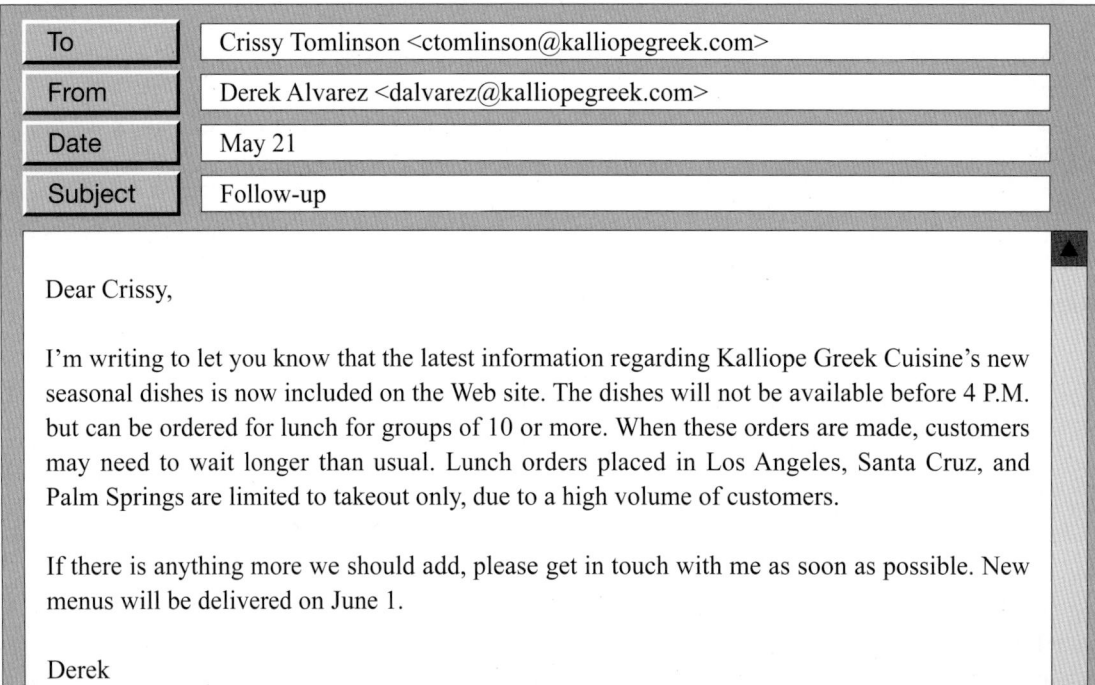

To	Crissy Tomlinson <ctomlinson@kalliopegreek.com>
From	Derek Alvarez <dalvarez@kalliopegreek.com>
Date	May 21
Subject	Follow-up

Dear Crissy,

I'm writing to let you know that the latest information regarding Kalliope Greek Cuisine's new seasonal dishes is now included on the Web site. The dishes will not be available before 4 P.M. but can be ordered for lunch for groups of 10 or more. When these orders are made, customers may need to wait longer than usual. Lunch orders placed in Los Angeles, Santa Cruz, and Palm Springs are limited to takeout only, due to a high volume of customers.

If there is anything more we should add, please get in touch with me as soon as possible. New menus will be delivered on June 1.

Derek

149. Why was the e-mail sent?

(A) To advertise a new business
(B) To report on some food items
(C) To check the status of an order
(D) To inquire about a meal preference

150. What is suggested about Kalliope Greek Cuisine?

(A) It no longer offers a seasonal menu.
(B) It provides a discount for takeout orders.
(C) It operates in multiple locations.
(D) It opens on weekdays at 4 P.M.

Questions 151-152 refer to the following e-mail.

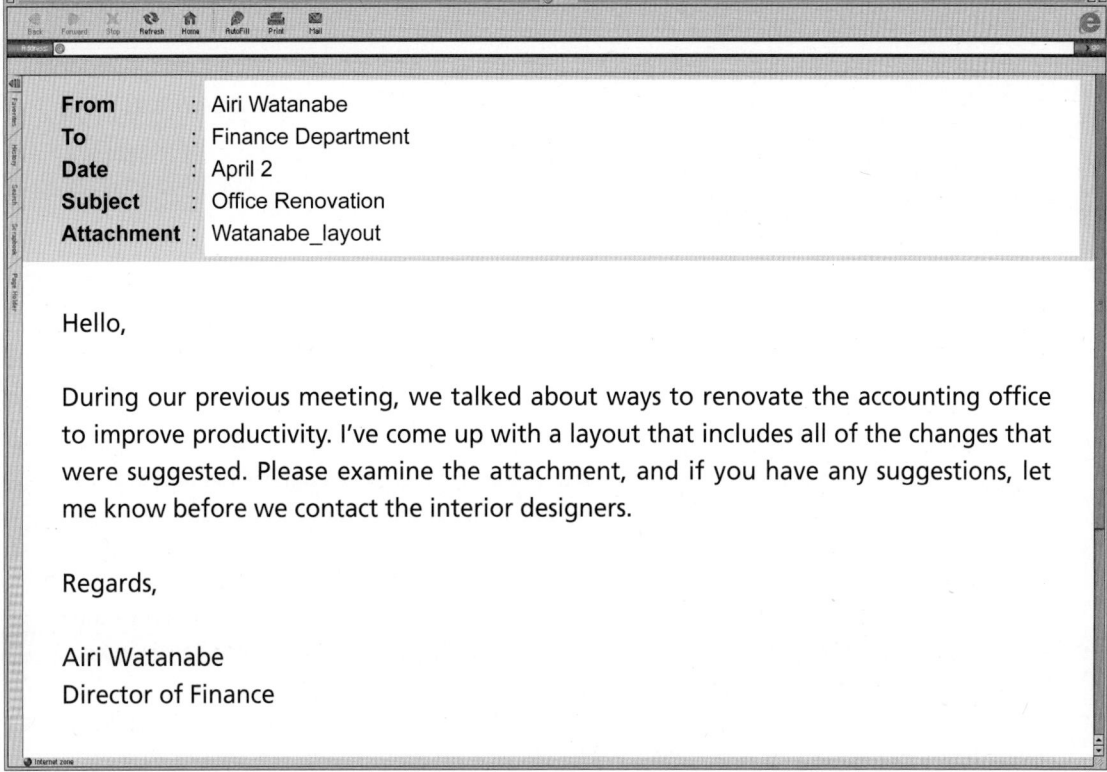

151. What is the purpose of the e-mail?

(A) To offer suggestions to a contract
(B) To review costs for office supplies
(C) To provide an update on a project discussed at a meeting
(D) To request a list of experienced design firms

152. What does Ms. Watanabe ask recipients to do with the attached document?

(A) Sign it and email it to a design company
(B) Print it and send it to the Finance Department
(C) Distribute copies to senior staff members
(D) Review it and give some feedback

GO ON TO THE NEXT PAGE

Questions 153-155 refer to the following advertisement.

Looking for some fun? Check out Alta Cima, this year's winner of *Entertain Around*'s "Most Incredible Spot."

Alta Cima Has Something for Everyone:

Beautiful Scenery
Beautiful all year long, Viloma Forest is home to hundreds of plants and animals. Walk around more than 20km of shady trails that surround our property. Pick up a map at the information kiosk or explore with our nature guides.

Games and Activities
Let loose by riding our exciting roller coasters, bumper cars, and Ferris wheel. Play carnival games outside or come indoors for a full arcade experience. On summer evenings, you can watch a fireworks show and a concert, or rent a boat to go out to the lake and fish.

History and Culture
If you are interested in the past, spend an afternoon in our Culture Hub. We provide various historical plays featuring both local and famous actors. We also have a reading center, where you can pick up educational materials to take home with you.

Every activity at Alta Cima is included in the price of a one-day package, excluding guided tours. Please call our information hotline for pricing details.

153. What most likely is Alta Cima?

(A) A historical park
(B) A concert hall
(C) A wildlife preserve
(D) A travel resort

154. What is mentioned about Alta Cima?

(A) It has a gift shop.
(B) It is located near the mountains.
(C) It received an award.
(D) It is operated by a famous actor.

155. What is offered at an additional cost?

(A) Carnival admission
(B) Music shows
(C) Guided tours
(D) Use of boats

Questions 156-158 refer to the following e-mail.

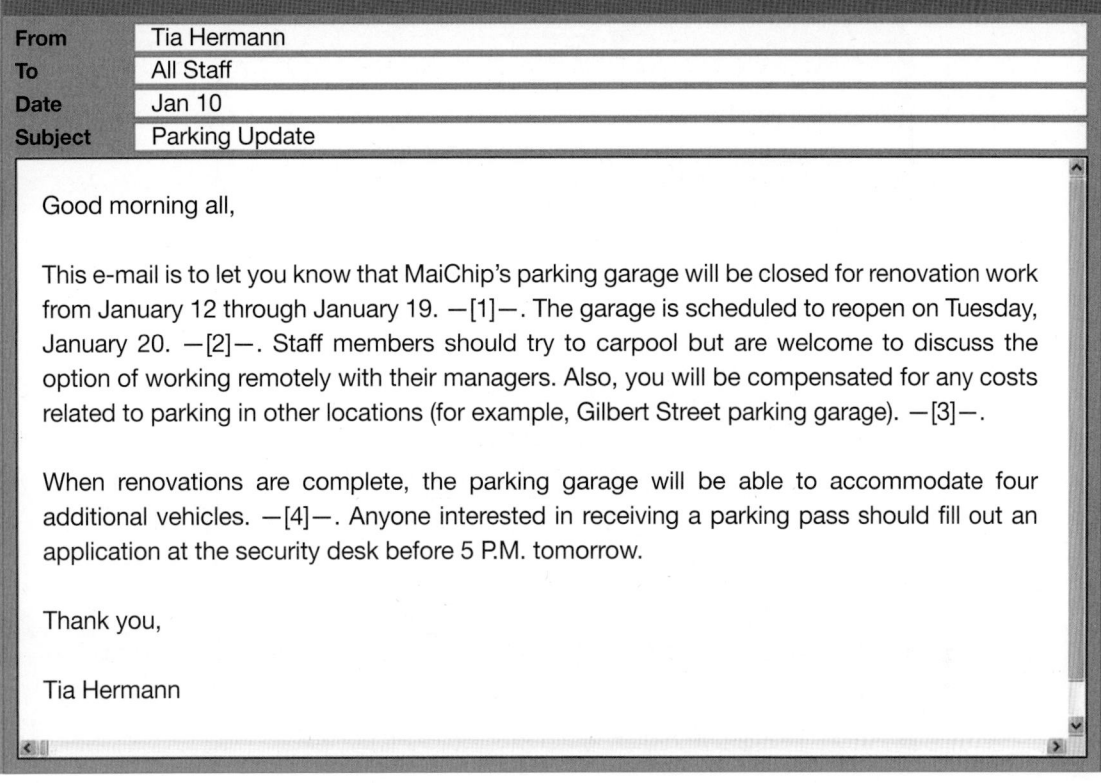

156. According to the e-mail, what can the staff talk to their supervisors about?

(A) Planning a carpool schedule
(B) The cheapest locations to park
(C) The option of telecommuting
(D) Filling out an application form

157. What is implied about the Gilbert Street parking garage?

(A) It was expanded recently.
(B) It is located far from MaiChip's office.
(C) It will be unavailable on January 20.
(D) It charges a fee.

158. In which of the positions marked [1], [2], [3], and [4] does the following sentence best belong?

"Additional lighting will be added, and the top floor will be covered."

(A) [1]
(B) [2]
(C) [3]
(D) [4]

Questions 159-160 refer to the following text message chain.

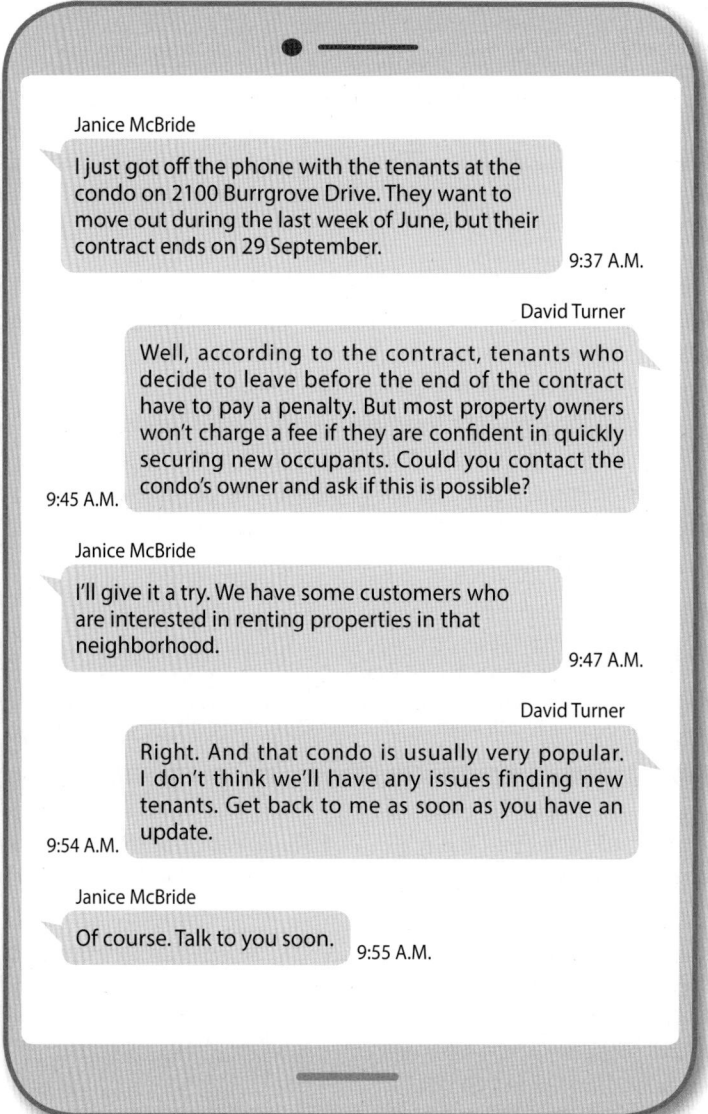

159. What do the tenants want to do?

(A) Buy a property
(B) Discuss a maintenance issue
(C) Cancel a contract early
(D) Find a more affordable condo

160. At 9:47 A.M., what does Ms. McBride most likely mean when she writes, "I'll give it a try"?

(A) She will convince the tenants to stay longer.
(B) She wants to renovate a building.
(C) She wants to negotiate a rental fee.
(D) She will talk to a property owner.

Questions 161-164 refer to the following Web page.

http://www.ferrytoncc.org

Ferryton Cultural Center
Autumn in the Spotlight!

Take time this fall to catch the new displays at the Ferryton Cultural Center. Enjoy the return of evening hours as summer comes to an end. We are also pleased to host free discussions with our artists and scholars.

Cultural Center Hours
Monday through Thursday: 9 A.M. – 5 P.M.
Saturday and Sunday: 9 A.M. – 7 P.M.
Closed Fridays

Autumn Displays
- Lives of the Colonists: Paper Correspondences
- Lisa Sheppard: History in Color
- Showcase of 15th-century tribal artifacts from our permanent collection

Panel Discussions
2 P.M. on September 22
Allan Koestner, a curator from Westville's Preservation Society, will visit to give a presentation about late 17th-century writer Boris Vishnievski, whose historic writings are on loan through the fall.

4:30 P.M. on October 13
Center Director Alice Nguyen will co-host a question and answer session about the city's preserved photograph library with professional photographer Lisa Sheppard. Ms. Sheppard will then give a presentation about her latest exhibition.

5 P.M. on November 7
Archaeologist Keith Dyrhaug will present a variety of native hunting and cooking artifacts that were just discovered around Ferryton and explain what we know about the people who lived here long ago. The pieces will be displayed in our main gallery starting November 1.

---

161. What is indicated about the Ferryton Cultural Center?

(A) Its discussion events charge an admission fee.
(B) It hires only local professionals.
(C) It closes later on weekends.
(D) Its director is a sculptor.

162. What is NOT mentioned as a part of the Ferryton Cultural Center's displays?

(A) Unique sculptures
(B) Ancient tools
(C) Preserved letters
(D) Historic photos

163. Who is Ms. Sheppard?

(A) An exhibitor
(B) A head curator
(C) An archaeologist
(D) A university professor

164. What will the November presentation be about?

(A) A scholar's research career
(B) Art techniques
(C) An image library
(D) Recent archaeological findings

Questions 165-168 refer to the following online chat discussion.

Jason Yi [1:23 P.M.]
Good afternoon. This is Jason with Hasbreve Electronics. I'm messaging you about the work request (AJS89) for your broken air conditioning unit. I'm available to look at it today between 3 and 6 P.M. Will you be available?

Chas del Torre [1:25 P.M.]
Sure, but I'm planning to run some errands. Could you give me a more specific time?

Jason Yi [1:26 P.M.]
I will be repairing units in Quimblydale and Barreston before coming to service yours. I can message you when I finish. That will give you about 30 minutes' notice.

Chas del Torre [1:29 P.M.]
Great! That would be very helpful.

Jason Yi [1:31 P.M.]
A colleague will be coming with me to your office. While I do the repair work, she will be observing and taking notes on how to replace a fan motor.

Chas del Torre [1:32 P.M.]
That shouldn't be a problem.

Jason Yi [1:33 P.M.]
Could you confirm your address for me? I have you listed at 632 West Lakeshore Drive.

Chas del Torre [1:34 P.M.]
That's right. See you this afternoon.

165. Who most likely is Mr. Yi?

    (A) A call center employee
    (B) A facilities supervisor
    (C) A service technician
    (D) A car salesperson

166. What is indicated about Mr. Yi?

    (A) He has relocated to a new city.
    (B) He has several appointments today.
    (C) He works only in the afternoon.
    (D) He will order a replacement part.

167. What is mentioned about Mr. Yi's colleague?

    (A) She will pick up some equipment.
    (B) She will watch a procedure.
    (C) She will bring some paperwork.
    (D) She will perform her job without any help.

168. At 1:29 P.M., what does Mr. del Torre most likely mean when he writes, "That would be very helpful"?

    (A) He plans to request a 30-minute consultation.
    (B) He cannot leave until the fan motor is fixed.
    (C) He recommends that some workers come early.
    (D) He wants Mr. Yi to send a message before arriving for an appointment.

Questions 169-171 refer to the following e-mail.

To	Jesse Schweizer <jschewizer@bookmarket.com>
From	Marcus Radic <mradic@sandiegosfcon.com>
Date	May 16
Subject	Re: Science Fiction Convention

Dear Ms. Schweizer,

This is to notify you that the San Diego Science Fiction Convention will no longer be held from June 12 to 15 as originally scheduled. The San Diego Convention Center is undergoing renovations, which are taking longer than originally planned. Therefore, we are pushing the convention dates back to July 28 to 31.

Your scheduled seminar, E-book Marketing for Independent Publishers, is now slated to take place on July 30. We are aware that this may cause inconvenience with your travel plans, and we are very sorry if this is the case.

Our dedicated convention volunteers are working to facilitate the process of rearranging our presenters' transportation and accommodations for the new dates. Please respond to this e-mail to let me know if the new dates are acceptable for you, and we will plan a revised itinerary and send you the updated convention schedule.

Sincerely,

Marcus Radic
San Diego Science Fiction Convention Planner

169. What is the purpose of the e-mail?

(A) To offer Ms. Schweizer a hotel room upgrade
(B) To ask Ms. Schweizer to review a budget proposal
(C) To request that Ms. Schweizer complete a survey
(D) To inform Ms. Schweizer of a scheduling change

170. What most likely is Ms. Schweizer's specialty?

(A) Event planning
(B) Travel management
(C) Book publishing
(D) Web design

171. What does Mr. Radic ask Ms. Schweizer to do?

(A) Give an opening speech
(B) Confirm her availability
(C) Submit a registration fee
(D) Join a panel of judges

Questions 172-175 refer to the following article.

Darsyville Tunnel Completed with Special Machines
by Kayla Luciano
September 2

Almost four years ago, work started on a double-decker tunnel from Darsyville to nearby Cloverton, on the other side of the Dunham Mountains. It was designed to be a direct link between our two cities. —[1]—. The work's lower costs were the direct result of two HRI-76 tunnel construction machines, made by Han-Ross Boring, a company based in Germany.

The two identical machines were leased from a private construction company, Sanaro Global. One was assembled right outside the city of Cloverton, while the other was set up on the west side of Darsyville city limits. —[2]—. The second machine posed some special challenges as it had to be assembled in a wooded area with no easy access to existing roads.

"Big tunneling projects are almost always going to run into some difficulties that must be overcome," explained Mina Jarvi, lead Sanaro Global engineer. —[3]—. In the case of this project, workers discovered that the exposed rock tested during the feasibility study was much softer than the rock underneath the mountain. This required bringing in special 57-ton plates capable of cutting through the harder stone. —[4]—. Engineers checked daily and found that the HRI-76s handled the extra workload well once the plates were attached.

Now, the tunnel is the region's economic centerpiece, providing better options for public transport, logistics, and tourism between the two cities. Some were concerned about the tunnel's appearance, but even they are pleased with the final result. Its entrances were sculpted to portray the beauty of the Dunham Mountain Range. All features, including a rail line, roadways, and a special lane for buses, improve transportation between the towns, making the tunnel a better alternative for companies that rely on trucking and freight train deliveries.

172. What is suggested about the HRI-76 machines?

(A) They belong to Han-Ross Boring.
(B) They were specially designed to dig the Darsyville Tunnel.
(C) They each weigh less than 57 tons.
(D) They were put together at the Darsyville Tunnel construction site.

173. What is indicated about Ms. Jarvi?

(A) She stopped working on the Darsyville Tunnel due to budget issues.
(B) Her work focuses only on tunnel digging.
(C) Her main job as lead engineer was repairing machinery.
(D) She thinks that projects like the Darsyville Tunnel usually involve challenges.

174. What is NOT suggested about the Darsyville Tunnel?

(A) It required more than four years to build.
(B) It is a more direct route to Cloverton.
(C) It was designed for trains and other vehicles.
(D) It was decorated to match the natural surroundings.

175. In which of the positions marked [1], [2], [3], and [4] does the following sentence best belong?

"The project, which was budgeted for 2.7 million dollars, was completed using just 2 million."

(A) [1]
(B) [2]
(C) [3]
(D) [4]

GO ON TO THE NEXT PAGE

Questions 176-180 refer to the following e-mail and invoice.

To	j.lazsco@txmail.com
From	info@savaboutique.com
Date	Wednesday, March 21
Subject	Off the rack! These clothes won't be here long!

Dear Mr. Lazsco,

Spring is almost here! That means that it's time once again to put our remaining winter clothes on sale. These unique styles won't be sold at such low prices again, so this is your last chance to buy fashionable apparel that holds up against even the harshest cold. Our yearly clearance catalog will soon be mailed out, but you can get a head start by going to our Web site and browsing through the electronic version. Shopping at our Web site is the best way to get the clothes you like before they are all gone. Plus, we are offering complimentary shipping for any orders that are made before April 2! And for purchases of $100 or more, we'll send you a coupon good for $10 at any retail store. Don't miss out on this amazing promotion!

Sue Mendoza, Director of Sales
Sava Boutique, Los Angeles

Important: This e-mail was sent because of your previous orders with us. Should you wish to leave this mailing list, just respond to this message with the word "unsubscribe" in the body.

Dear Mr. Lazsco,

We appreciate your order. The items in the order summary below will arrive in 4-8 business days. Remember that all purchases are final.

Order Number: 3423
Date: 1 April, 4:23 P.M.

Item No.	Description	Quantity	Total
6512	Snowflake bracelet with name inscription	1	$19
4778	Dark charcoal coat	1	$35
6581	Flannel pants (large)	1	$27

Subtotal	$81.00
2.9% tax	$2.35
Shipping	$0.00
Total	$83.35

176. Why would customers use the electronic catalog instead of the print catalog?

(A) To receive the most accurate pricing list
(B) To browse through more merchandise
(C) To buy items before they sell out
(D) To avoid paying extra for a mail catalog

177. What is most likely true about Mr. Lazsco?

(A) He recently made a large purchase.
(B) He has done business with Sava Boutique before.
(C) He is currently taking fashion courses.
(D) He runs a clothing store in Los Angeles.

178. What is indicated about the items ordered?

(A) They are made by famous designers.
(B) They will be sent later than expected.
(C) They come in only one color.
(D) They cannot be returned.

179. How could Mr. Lazsco have benefitted from an additional special offer?

(A) By applying a special promotion code
(B) By ordering earlier in the day
(C) By spending more money
(D) By going to an offline location instead

180. What is NOT indicated about Sava Boutique?

(A) It sells customized accessories.
(B) It uses a mailing list for customers.
(C) It offers seasonal discounts.
(D) It provides overnight delivery.

GO ON TO THE NEXT PAGE

Questions 181-185 refer to the following flyer and application.

Bonnie Acres
Delicious, Top-quality Produce Delivered to Your Door!

You are invited to join the Bonnie Acres Premium Club. Our members receive fresh, seasonal ingredients grown on our farm between April and October, as well as recipes created by top chefs.

Sign up for a Premium Package to get the following:
★ Weekly deliveries selected from over 50 kinds of in-season fruits, vegetables, and fresh assortments of herbs hand-picked by our staff.
★ Visit our farm once a week to pick fresh berries, peaches, and more.
★ Access our members' section on our Web site to read the latest farm news and find different recipes to try out.
★ Get a special discount to all Bonnie Acres events, including the Autumn Pumpkin Carnival. Normally $20.00, our members pay only $5!

Premium Club members receive a weekly package delivered to their doors. A Premium Family package costs $400, and a Premium Solo package is $200. Premium Solo members receive enough ingredients for 14 meals, whereas Premium Family packages come with enough for 21 meals.

All our produce is grown without the aid of toxic chemicals or insecticides. Only eco-friendly fertilizers are used on our fields. To learn more about us or to sign up for a membership, visit www.bonnieacres.com.

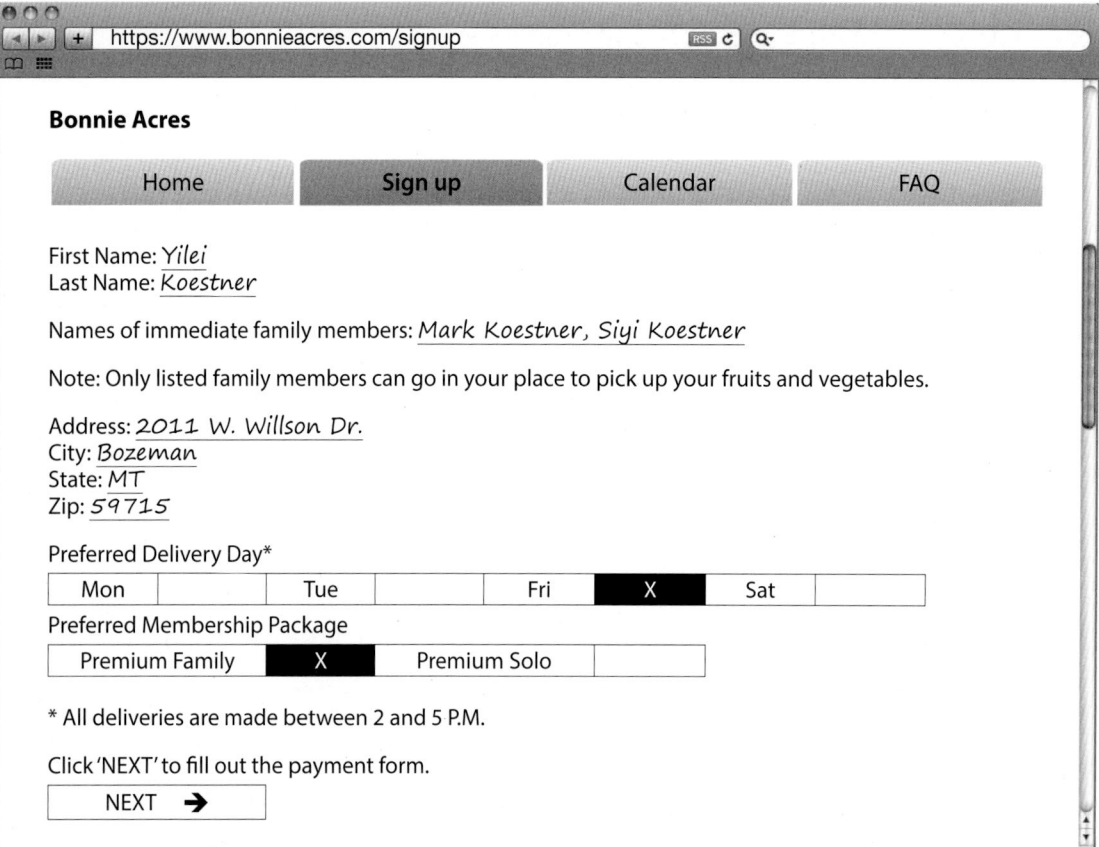

181. What is the purpose of the flyer?

(A) To announce a monthly sales event
(B) To advertise a membership program
(C) To share tips for food preparation
(D) To promote new organic produce

182. What is suggested about the employees at Bonnie Acres?

(A) They publish a cookbook every year.
(B) They post on the Bonnie Acres Web site daily.
(C) They gather produce from April to October.
(D) They ship produce to many grocery stores.

183. What is NOT indicated about Bonnie Acres?

(A) It holds an event in the fall.
(B) It hosts a cooking show.
(C) It applies environmentally-friendly fertilizers.
(D) It gives news updates online.

184. What is true about Ms. Koestner's membership?

(A) She will receive deliveries on Mondays.
(B) She can pick fruit on the farm.
(C) She is the only one allowed to pick up her own vegetables.
(D) She must pick up her items after 5 P.M.

185. How much should Ms. Koestner pay for the membership?

(A) $5
(B) $20
(C) $200
(D) $400

GO ON TO THE NEXT PAGE

Questions 186-190 refer to the following Web pages and e-mail.

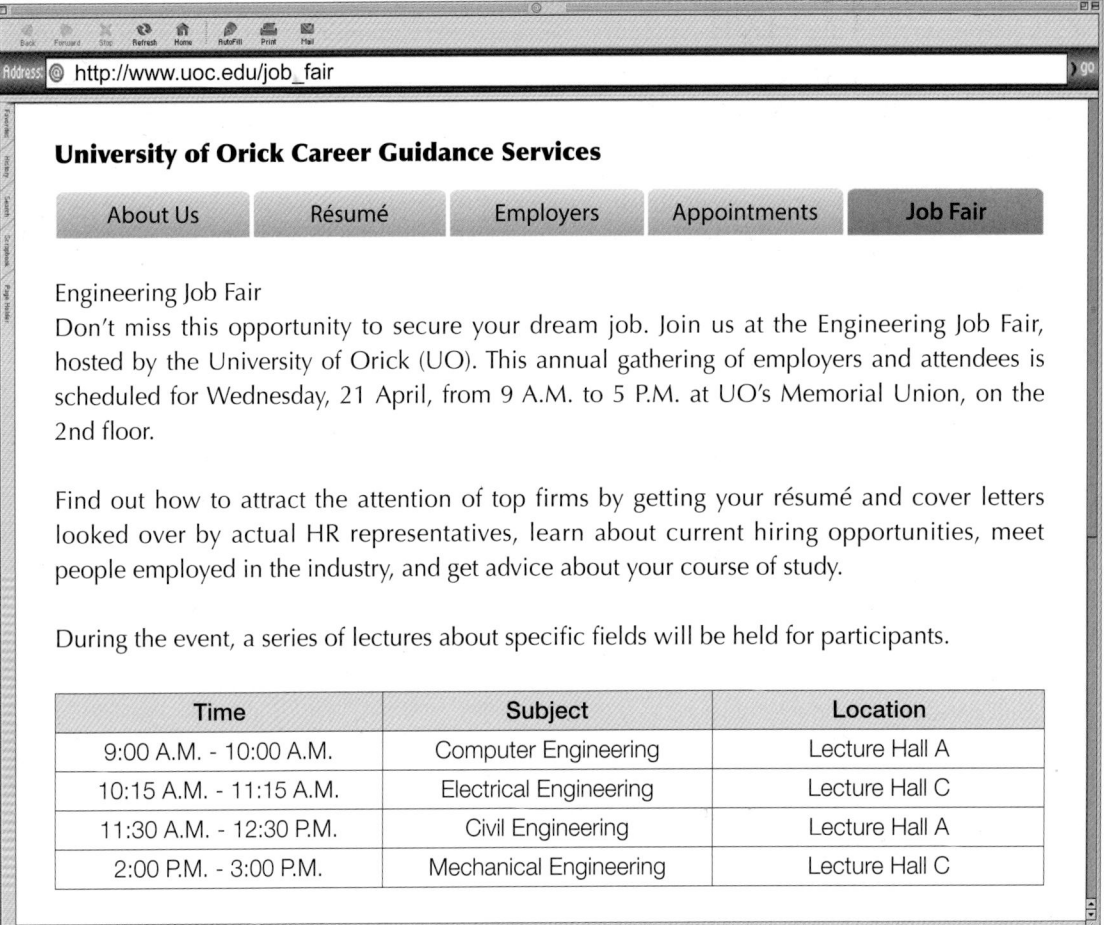

http://www.uoc.edu/job_fair

University of Orick Career Guidance Services

About Us | Résumé | Employers | Appointments | **Job Fair**

Engineering Job Fair

Don't miss this opportunity to secure your dream job. Join us at the Engineering Job Fair, hosted by the University of Orick (UO). This annual gathering of employers and attendees is scheduled for Wednesday, 21 April, from 9 A.M. to 5 P.M. at UO's Memorial Union, on the 2nd floor.

Find out how to attract the attention of top firms by getting your résumé and cover letters looked over by actual HR representatives, learn about current hiring opportunities, meet people employed in the industry, and get advice about your course of study.

During the event, a series of lectures about specific fields will be held for participants.

Time	Subject	Location
9:00 A.M. - 10:00 A.M.	Computer Engineering	Lecture Hall A
10:15 A.M. - 11:15 A.M.	Electrical Engineering	Lecture Hall C
11:30 A.M. - 12:30 P.M.	Civil Engineering	Lecture Hall A
2:00 P.M. - 3:00 P.M.	Mechanical Engineering	Lecture Hall C

To	Elise Amos
From	Daniel Han
Date	April 9
Subject	Help request

I will be giving a speech about my role here at Davis & Associates at the University of Orick in 12 days. I will be staying with some friends who live in the area, so accommodations won't be necessary. I'll also get a ride back to Berkeley with them that Friday. So I just need you to reserve me a one-way ticket for Wednesday, April 21. To allow preparation time for my 11:30 A.M. talk, I want to get to Orick between 9:30 A.M. and 10:00 A.M. As I will have a heavy bag, I don't want to transfer buses. In addition, due to my limited budget, the ticket price should be less than $60.

Thank you in advance for your help.

Daniel Han, Senior Engineer

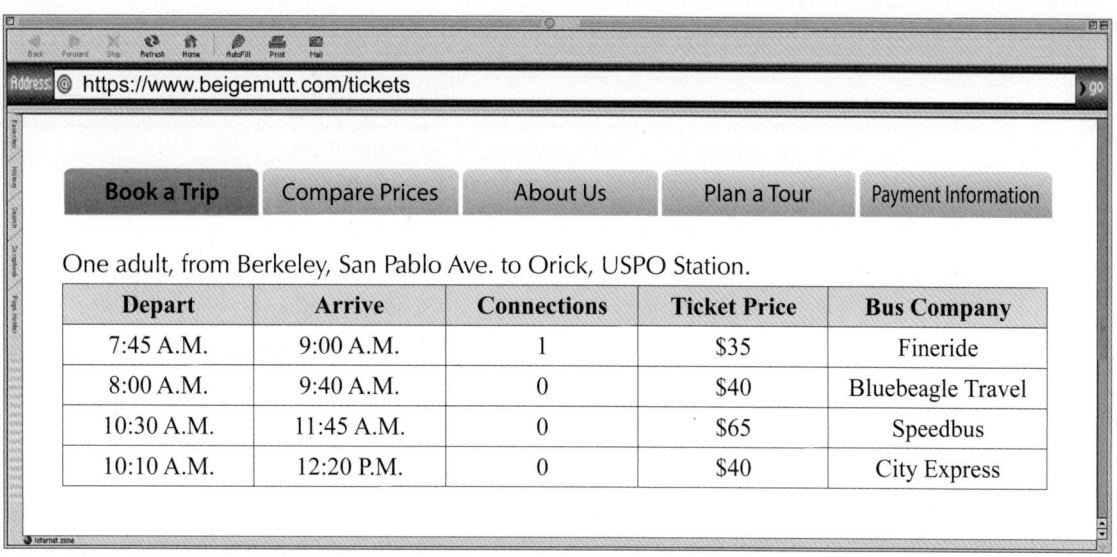

186. In the first Web page, the word "secure" in paragraph 1, line 1, is closest in meaning to
    (A) guard
    (B) attach
    (C) confirm
    (D) acquire

187. In the first Web page, what is NOT mentioned as a benefit of the job fair?
    (A) Consultations on current studies
    (B) Meetings with university professors
    (C) Reviews of job application documents
    (D) Information about open positions

188. Who most likely is Ms. Amos?
    (A) Mr. Han's student
    (B) An accounting manager
    (C) Mr. Han's assistant
    (D) A job fair organizer

189. In what field does Mr. Han work?
    (A) Computer engineering
    (B) Electrical engineering
    (C) Civil engineering
    (D) Mechanical engineering

190. What bus company will Mr. Han probably use to travel to Orick?
    (A) Fineride
    (B) Bluebeagle Travel
    (C) Speedbus
    (D) City Express

GO ON TO THE NEXT PAGE

39

Questions 191-195 refer to the following advertisement, e-mail, and invoice.

Temecula Winery Association (TWA) Promotion

As autumn approaches, are you looking for something fun to do? Try our weekend wine tour package, with discounted room rates and free admission to one of three local vineyards: Rancho California Orchard, Allison Spring Vineyard, or the Breaux Farm. You also get to take home samples from any one of those vineyards' wineries. We are working with Inland Tours to make this exclusive offer. You will also receive a framed photograph of you and your family in an optional hot-air balloon ride. To find out about pricing or to book rooms, please visit the following Web site: www.inlandtours951.com/winecountry_promo. This special event is available only to TWA members, from September 3 to November 12. To schedule your winery experience, email Inland Tours at least seven days in advance. A complimentary shuttle service is available to and from San Diego Airport, and reasonably-priced arrangements can be made for other nearby cities' airports as well.

To :	Beatrice Xao
From :	Caitlin Dubois
Date :	November 28
Subject :	Temecula Winery Association Tour — Samples and Billing
Attachment :	Wine Country Package Bill

Dear Ms. Xao,

The samples from the wine country package tour your association's members participated in have been packaged and shipped, along with the framed photographs. Attached to this e-mail is a final bill for all of the expenses. Please take note of the additional expense, which you cleared at the time, to cover the taxi service from John Wayne Airport on September 3. As you may remember, the Harrington family chose to take a flight arriving at that location.

Twenty-two of the other participants went on the tour of Rancho California Orchard, sixteen to Allison Spring Vineyard, but just four to the Breaux Farm. In the future, perhaps we should consider an alternative to Breaux.

Regards,

Caitlin Dubois

Inland Tours Invoice
Hemet, CA 92544
Date: November 28
Bill to: Temecula Winery Association

Description	Quantity	Rate	Subtotal
Wine Production	42	$40	$1,680
Frames	42	$4	$168
Transport	1	$250	$250
Shipping	42	$12	$504
		Total	$2,602

191. According to the advertisement, what is NOT included in the promotional tour package?

(A) Entry to a local business
(B) A complimentary meal
(C) Free product samples
(D) Discounts on accommodations

192. What is suggested about the Harrington family?

(A) They were visiting from a different country.
(B) They had their pictures taken in San Diego.
(C) They purchased additional Breaux Farm products.
(D) They contacted Inland Tours in August.

193. In the e-mail, the word "cleared" in paragraph 1, line 4, is closest in meaning to

(A) authorized
(B) released
(C) erased
(D) clarified

194. What does Ms. Dubois suggest?

(A) That a new summer tour be added
(B) That Rancho California Orchard increase its rates
(C) That a promotional deal be offered again
(D) That a different business be chosen

195. Why was Temecula Winery Association charged a fee of $250 by Inland Tours?

(A) Ms. Xao shipped souvenir sets to Inland Tours.
(B) Ms. Xao extended her tour package.
(C) The Harrington family requested a pickup service from the John Wayne Airport.
(D) The Harrington family visited all three tour locations.

GO ON TO THE NEXT PAGE

Questions 196-200 refer to the following brochure, class description, and phone message.

Xian-Harrington Design (XHD) is pleased to announce:
DIY Tile Installation Class
Led by Caitlin Xian
Price: $200

Starting April 20, this class will run for five weeks on Friday afternoons from 3:30 P.M. to 5:00 P.M. Beginners are welcome, but the course is restricted to community members that belong to the Homeowners Association.

Familiarize yourself with the process of laying down tile flooring and finish with a newfound confidence in your home improvement abilities. Skills that will be taught include cutting and attaching underlayment, tile sizing, mortar application, and grouting. Select from a wide assortment of tiles to design your own patterns.

Equipment and supplies can be purchased for about $150 directly from XHD. Not everything needs to be bought before the class begins, as each week's class will use different materials and tools, allowing students to spread out the cost. Although there are many different vendors that can supply the needed materials, please be attentive to product quality. Using high-quality materials and tools will ensure the best results.

DIY Tile Installation Class

Week	Topic	Materials
1	Equipment use and safety precautions, tile cutting practice	Protective eyewear, pencil, measuring tape
2	Choosing tiles and designing a pattern	Sketchbook, pen, tiles
3	Measuring and cutting tiles to size	Protective eyewear, triangle, scoring knife
4	Mixing and applying mortar	Trowel, putty blade, tile spacers, mixing bucket
5	Grouting and sealing	Grout, sponge

Please note that Xian-Harrington Design's workshop is open Saturdays from 9:00 A.M. to 2:00 P.M. for those who would like extra practice with the instructor regarding any of the techniques taught during the course. If you would like to schedule time with an instructor in our workshop outside this time, please call beforehand. Otherwise, you will need to be prepared to work on your own.

MESSAGE
Time: 1:00 P.M., Tuesday
For: Caitlin Xian
☑ Call ☐ Voice Message ☐ In-person visit

Notes:
Ray Elhassen called while you were out. He is registered for your class. He would like to know if the scoring knife that he already owns will be suitable for the class. I let him know that you would return his call when you get back. He can be reached at 555-9242.

196. What is suggested about the materials used in the DIY Tile Installation Class?

(A) Their price is lower than materials for other classes.
(B) They have to be ordered from a hardware store.
(C) They are included in the registration fee.
(D) They do not have to be bought at the same time.

197. In the brochure, the word "attentive" in paragraph 3, line 5, is closest in meaning to

(A) competent
(B) suspicious
(C) fascinated
(D) alert

198. What does the class description indicate?

(A) Xian-Harrington Design changed the location of its workshop recently.
(B) Xian-Harrington Design allows students to suggest future course topics.
(C) Instructors are available outside of the class hours.
(D) Some instructors may move their classes to Saturday morning.

199. What is suggested about Mr. Elhassen?

(A) He is a member of a local association.
(B) He has purchased extra materials for other students.
(C) He will be absent during the next course meeting.
(D) He frequently takes Xian-Harrington Design classes.

200. To which course session does the phone message most likely refer?

(A) Week 1
(B) Week 2
(C) Week 3
(D) Week 4

Stop! This is the end of the test. If you finish before time is called, you may go back to Part 5, 6, and 7 and check your work.

NO TEST MATERIAL ON THIS PAGE

NO TEST MATERIAL ON THIS PAGE

Answer Keys

MP3, 해석, 해설 온라인 무료 제공
모바일: QR코드 스캔을 통해 MP3 음원 바로 듣기 / 정답, 해석, 해설 바로 보기
PC: 파고다북스 사이트(www.pagodabook.com) 접속 / 로그인 후 다운로드

Listening Comprehension

1 (C)	2 (A)	3 (A)	4 (D)	5 (B)
6 (D)	7 (C)	8 (B)	9 (C)	10 (B)
11 (B)	12 (B)	13 (C)	14 (C)	15 (A)
16 (C)	17 (C)	18 (A)	19 (C)	20 (C)
21 (A)	22 (B)	23 (B)	24 (B)	25 (A)
26 (C)	27 (B)	28 (C)	29 (A)	30 (C)
31 (B)	32 (D)	33 (A)	34 (B)	35 (B)
36 (D)	37 (D)	38 (D)	39 (C)	40 (A)
41 (D)	42 (A)	43 (B)	44 (C)	45 (B)
46 (D)	47 (B)	48 (A)	49 (A)	50 (D)
51 (A)	52 (D)	53 (A)	54 (B)	55 (A)
56 (B)	57 (A)	58 (D)	59 (C)	60 (A)
61 (A)	62 (A)	63 (C)	64 (B)	65 (A)
66 (D)	67 (A)	68 (A)	69 (C)	70 (A)
71 (D)	72 (A)	73 (A)	74 (B)	75 (D)
76 (A)	77 (A)	78 (C)	79 (D)	80 (A)
81 (D)	82 (D)	83 (B)	84 (A)	85 (B)
86 (A)	87 (D)	88 (A)	89 (A)	90 (B)
91 (C)	92 (D)	93 (D)	94 (C)	95 (D)
96 (B)	97 (B)	98 (C)	99 (B)	100 (A)

Reading Comprehension

101 (A)	102 (C)	103 (C)	104 (D)	105 (B)
106 (A)	107 (C)	108 (D)	109 (A)	110 (A)
111 (A)	112 (D)	113 (B)	114 (B)	115 (B)
116 (B)	117 (A)	118 (B)	119 (A)	120 (D)
121 (A)	122 (B)	123 (D)	124 (A)	125 (B)
126 (A)	127 (D)	128 (C)	129 (C)	130 (C)
131 (B)	132 (A)	133 (C)	134 (D)	135 (B)
136 (C)	137 (D)	138 (D)	139 (A)	140 (D)
141 (B)	142 (A)	143 (B)	144 (B)	145 (C)
146 (D)	147 (A)	148 (D)	149 (B)	150 (C)
151 (C)	152 (D)	153 (D)	154 (C)	155 (C)
156 (C)	157 (D)	158 (A)	159 (C)	160 (D)
161 (C)	162 (A)	163 (A)	164 (D)	165 (C)
166 (B)	167 (B)	168 (D)	169 (D)	170 (C)
171 (B)	172 (D)	173 (D)	174 (A)	175 (A)
176 (C)	177 (B)	178 (D)	179 (C)	180 (D)
181 (B)	182 (C)	183 (B)	184 (B)	185 (D)
186 (D)	187 (B)	188 (C)	189 (C)	190 (B)
191 (B)	192 (D)	193 (A)	194 (D)	195 (C)
196 (D)	197 (D)	198 (C)	199 (A)	200 (C)

초판 1쇄 인쇄 2018년 7월 4일
초판 1쇄 발행 2018년 7월 4일
초판 11쇄 발행 2024년 9월 30일

지 은 이 | 파고다교육그룹 언어교육연구소
펴 낸 이 | 박경실
펴 낸 곳 | **PAGODA Books** 파고다북스
출판등록 | 2005년 5월 27일 제 300-2005-90호
주   소 | 06614 서울특별시 서초구 강남대로 419, 19층(서초동, 파고다타워)
전   화 | (02) 6940-4070
팩   스 | (02) 536-0660
홈페이지 | www.pagodabook.com

저작권자 | ⓒ 2018 파고다아카데미

이 책의 저작권은 저자와 출판사에 있습니다. 서면에 의한 저작권자와 출판사의 허락 없이
내용의 일부 혹은 전부를 인용 및 복제하거나 발췌하는 것을 금합니다.

Copyright ⓒ 2018 by PAGODA Academy

All rights reserved. No part of this publication may be reproduced, stored
in a retrieval system, or transmitted, in any form, or by any means, electronic,
mechanical, photocopying, recording or otherwise, without the prior written
permission of the copyright holder and the publisher.

ISBN 978-89-6281-817-8 (13740)

파고다북스   www.pagodabook.com
파고다 어학원   www.pagoda21.com
파고다 인강   www.pagodastar.com
테스트 클리닉   www.testclinic.com

▎낙장 및 파본은 구매처에서 교환해 드립니다.

PAGODA Books

파고다토익 시험 직전 마무리 모의고사 Vol.2 TEST 3

해설 바로 보기   음원 바로 듣기

PAGODA Books

시험 진행 안내

❶ 시험 시간: 120분(2시간)
- Listening Comprehension 100문제: 45분
- Reading Comprehension 100문제: 75분
- L/C 진행 후 휴식 시간 없이 바로 R/C 진행

❷ 준비물
- 컴퓨터용 사인펜 또는 연필

❸ 시험 응시 준수 사항
- 시험 시작 10분 전 입실 (이후에는 입실 불가)
- 종료 30분 전과 10분 전에 시험 종료 공지함
- 휴대전화의 전원을 꺼둘 것

❹ OMR 답안지 표기 요령
- 반드시 컴퓨터용 사인펜 또는 연필로 표기
- 개인정보, 문제번호, 단체명, 문제번호, 학과(부서) 및 학번코드 표기
  (학과(부서)코드는 별도 공지)

※ 개인정보, 문제번호, 학과(부서)코드를 틀리게 표기했을 경우 채점 및 성적 확인이 불가능하므로 주의하시기 바랍니다.

답안 작성 요령 Sample

○	●	Ⓑ	Ⓒ	Ⓓ
×	Ⓐ	Ⓑ	ⓧ	Ⓓ
×	Ⓐ	Ⓑ	Ⓒ	Ⓓ
×	Ⓐ	Ⓑ	Ⓒ	Ⓓ
×	Ⓐ	Ⓑ	Ⓒ	Ⓓ

LISTENING TEST

In the Listening test, you will be asked to demonstrate how well you understand spoken English. The entire listening test will last approximately 45 minutes. There are four parts, and directions are given for each part. You must mark your answers on the separate answer sheet. Do not write your answers in your test book.

PART 1

Directions: For each question in this part, you will hear four statements about a picture in your test book. When you hear the statements, you must select the one statement that best describes what you see in the picture. Then find the number of the question on your answer sheet and mark your answer. The statements will not be printed in your test book and will be spoken only one time.

Statement (B), "A man is pointing at a document," is the best description of the picture, so you should select answer (B) and mark it on your answer sheet.

1.

2.

GO ON TO THE NEXT PAGE

3.

4.

5.

6.

GO ON TO THE NEXT PAGE

PART 2

Directions: You will hear a question or statement and three responses spoken in English. They will not be printed in your test book and will be spoken only one time. Select the best response to the question or statement and mark the letter (A), (B), or (C) on your answer sheet.

7. Mark your answer on your answer sheet.
8. Mark your answer on your answer sheet.
9. Mark your answer on your answer sheet.
10. Mark your answer on your answer sheet.
11. Mark your answer on your answer sheet.
12. Mark your answer on your answer sheet.
13. Mark your answer on your answer sheet.
14. Mark your answer on your answer sheet.
15. Mark your answer on your answer sheet.
16. Mark your answer on your answer sheet.
17. Mark your answer on your answer sheet.
18. Mark your answer on your answer sheet.
19. Mark your answer on your answer sheet.
20. Mark your answer on your answer sheet.
21. Mark your answer on your answer sheet.
22. Mark your answer on your answer sheet.
23. Mark your answer on your answer sheet.
24. Mark your answer on your answer sheet.
25. Mark your answer on your answer sheet.
26. Mark your answer on your answer sheet.
27. Mark your answer on your answer sheet.
28. Mark your answer on your answer sheet.
29. Mark your answer on your answer sheet.
30. Mark your answer on your answer sheet.
31. Mark your answer on your answer sheet.

PART 3

Directions: You will hear some conversations between two or more people. You will be asked to answer three questions about what the speakers say in each conversation. Select the best response to each question and mark the letter (A), (B), (C), or (D) on your answer sheet. The conversations will not be printed in your test book and will be spoken only one time.

32. What is the main subject of the conversation?

    (A) An assignment deadline
    (B) A color printer
    (C) A sales presentation
    (D) A potential client

33. What does the woman request?

    (A) An example document
    (B) A larger desk area
    (C) Some temporary employees
    (D) Better quality graphics

34. What does the man recommend the woman do?

    (A) Edit a handbook
    (B) Submit a form
    (C) Contact a coworker
    (D) File some paperwork

35. Where do the speakers work?

    (A) At a clothing retailer
    (B) At an advertising agency
    (C) At a graphic design firm
    (D) At a book store

36. What does the man ask Scarlett about?

    (A) Upgrading a system
    (B) Recruiting more employees
    (C) Changing a due date
    (D) Creating a survey

37. What does the man say he will do?

    (A) Send out an e-mail notification
    (B) Pass out some handouts
    (C) Hold a public forum
    (D) Draft a business plan

38. What does the woman request help with?

    (A) Booking a venue
    (B) Finding a train station
    (C) Completing a project
    (D) Arranging a trip

39. What does the man recommend asking a supervisor about?

    (A) A schedule
    (B) A budget
    (C) Some directions
    (D) Meal options

40. According to the man, what is provided?

    (A) Accommodation
    (B) Entertainment
    (C) Transportation
    (D) Food

41. What are the speakers talking about?

    (A) A laptop charger
    (B) A video editing software
    (C) A speaker system
    (D) An exercise device

42. What problem does the woman mention?

    (A) A program does not function properly.
    (B) A product test has been postponed.
    (C) More funds are necessary for a project.
    (D) Some components are missing.

43. What is the woman asked to do?

    (A) Send a report
    (B) Conduct a survey
    (C) Look over a user manual
    (D) Revise some sales figures

GO ON TO THE NEXT PAGE

44. What does the woman say will be held in one week?

(A) A department meeting
(B) A technology convention
(C) A product launch
(D) A retirement banquet

45. What is the man concerned about?

(A) Parking costs
(B) A late train
(C) Upcoming deadlines
(D) A small venue

46. Why does the woman say, "A taxi ride is only $15"?

(A) To point out that a fee is high
(B) To clarify a misunderstanding
(C) To offer a suggestion
(D) To show surprise

47. According to the woman, what was her company unable to do?

(A) Fix an engine
(B) Process a payment
(C) Find some files
(D) Send electronic messages

48. What does the woman offer to do for the man?

(A) Look into new travel arrangements
(B) Provide a discount voucher
(C) Issue a full refund
(D) Give him a seat upgrade

49. Why does the man have to leave soon?

(A) He has to participate in a conference.
(B) Inclement weather is anticipated.
(C) He needs to get on a connecting train.
(D) There is more traffic in the afternoon.

50. Where do the speakers most likely work?

(A) At a manufacturing plant
(B) At a Web design company
(C) At a recruiting agency
(D) At an appliance store

51. What is the problem?

(A) Sales have declined.
(B) A deadline was not met.
(C) Some merchandise was damaged.
(D) A computer system is not working.

52. What do the speakers decide to do?

(A) Improve the level of customer service
(B) Provide discount coupons
(C) Hire more experienced employees
(D) Place an advertisement in the newspaper

53. What does the woman like about the venue?

(A) It was recently renovated.
(B) It includes state-of-the-art equipment.
(C) It is close to public transportation.
(D) It is quite affordable.

54. What does the woman say about the event?

(A) It will have a large number of attendees.
(B) It will have food catered by a local restaurant.
(C) It will be held during the weekend.
(D) It will feature a famous speaker.

55. What does the man point out about the contract?

(A) It has to be modified.
(B) It mentions that a security guard must be present.
(C) It states that extra furniture can be provided.
(D) It must be submitted tomorrow.

56. What does the woman imply when she says, "I was just getting ready to go"?

(A) She cannot talk for very long.
(B) She is late for a meeting.
(C) She will start on an assignment tomorrow.
(D) She believes another coworker can help.

57. What is the man worried about?

(A) The appearance of a report
(B) The deadline of a project
(C) The price of a product
(D) The accuracy of a description

58. Why does the man apologize?

(A) He accidentally deleted an e-mail.
(B) He did not contact a client.
(C) He looked at an incorrect file.
(D) He forgot to get approval from a manager.

59. What are the speakers discussing?

(A) A building design
(B) A cafeteria menu
(C) A recent office move
(D) An annual budget

60. According to the man, what did the comments show?

(A) Board members were not pleased.
(B) Staff requires additional training.
(C) A firm should recruit more employees.
(D) Managers must hold frequent evaluations.

61. What will happen in November?

(A) A seminar will take place.
(B) A project will begin.
(C) Bonuses will be given.
(D) Contracts will be reviewed.

| Wallpaper Selections ||
Item Code	Color of Wallpaper
T504	Orange
S272	Crimson
C988	Copper
H305	Honey

62. How did the man reach his decision?

(A) He looked at some samples.
(B) He conducted research online.
(C) He compared some costs.
(D) He talked to a colleague.

63. Look at the graphic. Which item will the man most likely choose?

(A) T504
(B) S272
(C) C988
(D) H305

64. Why does the woman have to call back later?

(A) She needs to get a manager's approval.
(B) She has to review a work schedule.
(C) She must check some inventory first.
(D) She is meeting with another client.

GO ON TO THE NEXT PAGE

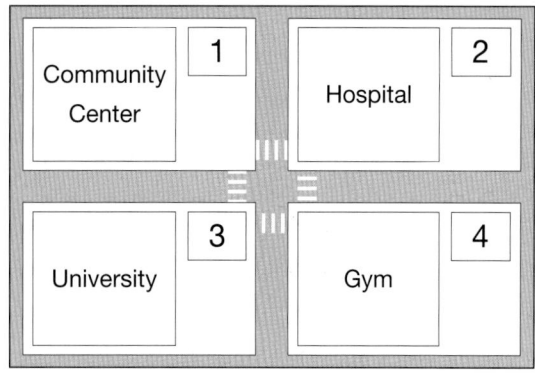

Sender's Name	Subject	Size
Kelly Mathers	Staff headcount	155 KB
Denise Shah	Marketing plan	3 MB
Lisa Redder	Budget estimate	30 KB
Maria Gonzales	Audit report	112 KB

65. What does the man want to avoid having near the store?

(A) Street vendors
(B) Traffic congestion
(C) Parking meters
(D) Loud noises

66. Look at the graphic. Which location do the speakers choose for their store?

(A) Location 1
(B) Location 2
(C) Location 3
(D) Location 4

67. What does the woman say she will do next?

(A) Order product samples
(B) Sign some paperwork
(C) Go to a work site
(D) Contact an agency

68. Look at the graphic. What is the name of the woman speaking?

(A) Kelly Mathers
(B) Denise Shah
(C) Lisa Redder
(D) Maria Gonzales

69. How will the man assist the woman?

(A) By emailing a supervisor
(B) By reviewing an itinerary
(C) By printing a file
(D) By placing an order

70. Why will the man be absent from a meeting?

(A) He will be interviewing some job candidates.
(B) He has to be present to receive a package.
(C) He is departing for a business trip.
(D) He must wait for a customer's call.

PART 4

Directions: You will hear some talks given by a single speaker. You will be asked to answer three questions about what the speaker says in each talk. Select the best response to each question and mark the letter (A), (B), (C), or (D) on your answer sheet. The talks will not be printed in your test book and will be spoken only one time.

71. Where is the announcement being made?

(A) At a fitness center
(B) At a convention center
(C) At a sporting goods store
(D) At a clothing factory

72. What can listeners find on the third floor?

(A) A training session
(B) Merchandise on sale
(C) A club gathering
(D) Snacks and beverages

73. What can listeners do until April 1?

(A) Provide feedback
(B) Register for a membership
(C) Pick up coupons
(D) Participate in a raffle

74. Where does the speaker work?

(A) At a camera shop
(B) At a video game maker
(C) At a computer retailer
(D) At a phone manufacturer

75. What will the video be about?

(A) Current technology trends
(B) Exclusive device features
(C) Innovative electronics companies
(D) Famous inventors

76. What are listeners asked to do?

(A) Fill out some documents
(B) Relocate to another building
(C) Review a script
(D) Wear some costumes

77. Where do the listeners most likely work?

(A) At a university
(B) At a recruiting agency
(C) At a construction company
(D) At a warehouse

78. What does the speaker recommend the listeners do?

(A) Manage their time better
(B) Take more breaks
(C) Discuss certain issues with employees
(D) Provide staff with frequent feedback

79. What will the speaker do next?

(A) Check the status of a shipment
(B) Talk about a personal experience
(C) Answer some questions
(D) Pass out some forms

80. Why has the meeting been called?

(A) To introduce a client
(B) To discuss a mistake
(C) To report on quarterly sales figures
(D) To review a packaging procedure

81. Why does the speaker say, "It's been 10 days"?

(A) To urge workers to hurry
(B) To thank the listeners for their patience
(C) To emphasize the popularity of an item
(D) To show concern about a situation

82. What does the speaker want Fadila to do?

(A) Confirm some information
(B) Contact a delivery company
(C) Prepare a presentation
(D) Arrange another shipment

GO ON TO THE NEXT PAGE

83. What is the topic of the seminar?

    (A) Job search skills
    (B) Public speaking techniques
    (C) Sales strategies
    (D) Script writing

84. What are participants invited to do after the seminar?

    (A) Attend a performance
    (B) Purchase study materials
    (C) Enroll in advanced classes
    (D) Talk to potential employers

85. What does the speaker recommend the listeners do?

    (A) Watch an online lecture
    (B) Sign up soon
    (C) Complete a survey
    (D) Contact a broadcasting network

86. What did the listeners agree to do?

    (A) Watch a recording
    (B) Fix some machinery
    (C) Oversee a conference
    (D) Try out a program

87. What does the speaker imply when he says, "you can't make a mistake here"?

    (A) The listeners don't need to worry about doing something wrong.
    (B) The listeners will have no difficulty with a task.
    (C) The listeners will be given extra help.
    (D) The listeners must follow instructions precisely.

88. What are the listeners instructed to do next?

    (A) Sign some paperwork
    (B) Create an account
    (C) Open a user guide
    (D) Move to another room

89. Why does the speaker apologize to the listeners?

    (A) She did not send a notification.
    (B) She set a tight deadline.
    (C) A last-minute change was made.
    (D) A project was too difficult.

90. What is the purpose of the meeting?

    (A) To revise an advertisement
    (B) To prepare for an event
    (C) To finalize a contract
    (D) To go over some expenses

91. Why does the speaker want to keep the meeting short?

    (A) She has to attend a training session.
    (B) She wants to spend more time on a demonstration.
    (C) An assignment must be submitted soon.
    (D) A client is visiting earlier than expected.

92. Where does the talk most likely take place?

    (A) At a department store
    (B) At a factory
    (C) At a cooking school
    (D) At a restaurant

93. Why does the speaker say, "this is a three-hour tour"?

    (A) He requests assistance from some listeners.
    (B) He is anticipating a cancellation.
    (C) He is warning the listeners.
    (D) He would like to revise some details.

94. According to the speaker, what should the listeners keep?

    (A) Their brochures
    (B) Their receipts
    (C) Their schedules
    (D) Their badges

Cedartown Building Elevator Directory	
A	2nd – 6th Floors
B	7th – 13th Floors
C	14th – 21st Floors
D	22nd – 28th Floors

Shelf 1 apples	Shelf 2 bananas	Shelf 3 grapefruits	Shelf 4 oranges

95. What will most likely be discussed at the meeting?

(A) A marketing campaign
(B) An employee evaluation
(C) A maintenance issue
(D) A remodeling project

96. What should the woman do at the front desk?

(A) Review a map
(B) Pick up some identification
(C) Drop off a package
(D) Obtain a parking pass

97. Look at the graphic. Which floor is the speaker's office located on?

(A) The 6th floor
(B) The 13th floor
(C) The 21st floor
(D) The 28th floor

98. What is the supermarket celebrating?

(A) A business reopening
(B) An employee's promotion
(C) A store anniversary
(D) A product launch

99. When will the event end?

(A) Tonight
(B) Tomorrow
(C) In three days
(D) This weekend

100. Look at the graphic. Which produce shelf contains items with an additional discount?

(A) Shelf 1
(B) Shelf 2
(C) Shelf 3
(D) Shelf 4

This is the end of the Listening test. Turn to Part 5 in your test book.

GO ON TO THE NEXT PAGE

15

READING TEST

In the Reading test, you will read a variety of texts and answer several different types of reading comprehension questions. The entire Reading test will last 75 minutes. There are three parts, and directions are given for each part. You are encouraged to answer as many questions as possible within the time allowed.

You must mark your answers on the separate answer sheet. Do not write your answers in your test book.

PART 5

Directions: A word or phrase is missing in each of the sentences below. Four answer choices are given below each sentence. Select the best answer to complete the sentence. Then mark the letter (A), (B), (C), or (D) on your answer sheet.

101. At Naxxo Tech, you may become a team leader if you have ------- two full years of work as an assistant technician.

(A) completed
(B) approved
(C) predicted
(D) terminated

102. A coworker of ------- will be attending the technology conference in France.

(A) I
(B) me
(C) my
(D) mine

103. Some of the items on our menu are subject to change ------- as they are dependent on supplier availability.

(A) properly
(B) nearly
(C) quarterly
(D) highly

104. Please join us in honoring Colin Hernandez, ------- of the Prize for Research in Behavioral Science.

(A) receiving
(B) recipient
(C) receives
(D) received

105. Examine ------- document in the folder thoroughly before sending them to the client.

(A) total
(B) full
(C) all
(D) each

106. Heather Langer began her ------- after selling the company she founded almost three decades ago.

(A) retirement
(B) retire
(C) retiring
(D) retired

107. Passengers are advised to arrive at the airport two hours ------- their flights are scheduled to depart.

(A) above
(B) before
(C) toward
(D) onto

108. Wales Ltd. has acquired Daoust Manufacturing for ------- 10 million pounds in cash and stock.

(A) approximate
(B) approximates
(C) approximation
(D) approximately

109. ------- receiving the Employee of the Year Award, Mr. Keyes made a point of thanking his manager.

(A) Upon
(B) Around
(C) Except
(D) Into

110. Make sure to include the new features of the oven when ------- the instruction manual.

(A) edited
(B) edits
(C) editing
(D) edit

111. SCU Solutions will open a new regional office in Kyoto to ------- the company's growth in Asia.

(A) designate
(B) accommodate
(C) relieve
(D) inspect

112. The Parks Manager noted that the visitors' center ------- open for the entire holiday weekend.

(A) to stay
(B) staying
(C) should stay
(D) that stays

113. Markton Motors has a ------- as an environmentally-friendly company that mainly manufactures electric cars.

(A) reputation
(B) generosity
(C) forecast
(D) testimonial

114. Since he is a new employee, Mr. Miller was ------- to comment on the problem with the company's product.

(A) reluctant
(B) reluctance
(C) reluctantly
(D) more reluctantly

115. A training course on the new inventory software will be held ------- the team meeting.

(A) when
(B) because
(C) following
(D) just

116. The building on Monroe Street has been ------- at double the amount it originally cost to construct.

(A) valued
(B) valuer
(C) valuation
(D) value

117. The new packaging machines have ------- Grant Pharmaceuticals to lower production costs.

(A) established
(B) developed
(C) enabled
(D) improved

118. Atom Star Technical Support requires its staff to deal with IT issues as ------- as possible.

(A) promptness
(B) promptest
(C) promptly
(D) prompter

119. Customers have limited time to take advantage of the special sale, as ------- lasts until June 30 only.

(A) we
(B) she
(C) they
(D) it

120. Jemaine Momoa is the first runner-up in the national culinary arts -------.

(A) competitor
(B) competition
(C) competitive
(D) competitively

GO ON TO THE NEXT PAGE

121. At Doremi Amusement Park, we take pride in friendly service, so please greet all visitors with -------.

(A) enthusiasm
(B) specification
(C) accomplishment
(D) improvement

122. The popularity of online lectures is ------- even though offline classes are still in demand.

(A) increase
(B) increases
(C) increased
(D) increasing

123. Heimat Department Store will expand its outdoor parking lot ------- build a new one.

(A) rather than
(B) with reference to
(C) such as
(D) initially

124. The remodeling of the lobby has to be postponed ------- the budget reduction confirmed last week by the board.

(A) in that case
(B) ahead of
(C) because of
(D) opposite from

125. The subway expansion project has local residents pleased with the ------- of decreased commute times.

(A) quotation
(B) consensus
(C) prospect
(D) pattern

126. ------- you have applied all of the editor's corrections to the article, the printing process will begin.

(A) Once
(B) Later
(C) Often
(D) First

127. The board of directors meeting concluded so ------- that only a few attendees were able to ask questions about the proposed merger.

(A) abruptly
(B) basically
(C) noticeably
(D) generally

128. If an employee loses their card key, the Maintenance Department will charge a replacement fee and issue -------.

(A) another
(B) one another
(C) other
(D) other one

129. Employees should frequently check the bulletin board on the company intranet to learn the status of any ------- initiatives.

(A) dependent
(B) restrictive
(C) practical
(D) pending

130. By the end of this year, the plant in Slovakia ------- at least 10,000 truck engines.

(A) will be built
(B) will have built
(C) has built
(D) has been built

PART 6

Directions: Read the texts that follow. A word, phrase, or sentence is missing in parts of each text. Four answer choices for each question are given below the text. Select the best answer to complete the text. Then mark the letter (A), (B), (C), or (D) on your answer sheet.

Questions 131-134 refer to the following advertisement.

My Castle Interior Decorators

My Castle creates interior designs with artwork and decorations to match any home, no matter how large. Our work has ------- small city apartments in addition to multi-million-dollar resorts and country estates. -------. However, no single firm can provide all the necessary supplies. That's why My Castle has created strong partnerships with specialized manufacturers ------- to supply us with the materials we require. These relationships give us the resources needed to fulfill any -------. That means that no matter what your dream home may look like, we can make it a reality.

131.
131. (A) contracted
(B) associated
(C) transformed
(D) regarded

132. (A) A limited warranty is offered for all of our work.
(B) Be aware that it can be difficult to decorate on a limited budget.
(C) Certain areas have strict laws concerning building modifications.
(D) We use our own supplies for the majority of our projects.

133. (A) prepared
(B) preparation
(C) prepares
(D) prepare

134. (A) research
(B) questionnaire
(C) form
(D) order

GO ON TO THE NEXT PAGE

Questions 135-138 refer to the following excerpt from a brochure.

Maple County Woodland Group

Our mission here at Maple County Woodland Group is to guard our public lands, protected forests, and private properties from plant diseases. We ------- inspect the health of our
135.
forests in Maple County. -------. We then prepare reports on forest conditions for national
136.
agencies, which allows us to lobby for healthy forest regulations.

------- a nonprofit organization, the Maple County Woodland Group needs your help and
137.
donations to accomplish our work. We rely on your aid to ------- our forests. Check out
138.
www.mcwgroup.org to volunteer, make a monetary pledge, or learn more about what we do.

135. (A) frequently
(B) frequent
(C) frequented
(D) frequents

136. (A) We are the biggest developer in the area focused on property sales.
(B) Doing so helps us to collect and analyze data on forest conditions.
(C) Also, we provide opportunities for day-long hiking tours.
(D) Recently, a forest protection law was passed.

137. (A) For
(B) Within
(C) Containing
(D) As

138. (A) increase
(B) control
(C) discover
(D) protect

Questions 139-142 refer to the following article.

Grandview Science Academy Gets Gift from Darryl McCurdie

A representative for Darryl McCurdie ------- that the renowned biologist has made a
                                         139.
considerable financial contribution for the planned renovation of the Grandview Science Academy. "Without Dr. McCurdie's generosity," said Academic Director Chris Walker, "it is unlikely that we would have been able to continue with our planned expansion of the school."

-------. Now, it will be possible to build new laboratories in the basement of the ------- school
140.   **141.**
building. The facilities will include a 25-table biology laboratory, state-of-the-art chemistry facilities, and a special demonstration area for science experiments. In addition, private study rooms will be made available ------- the first-floor lecture halls.
                                          142.

139. (A) has announced
(B) announce
(C) will announce
(D) announcement

140. (A) Therefore, the academy's facilities are now being used for community events.
(B) Dr. McCurdie's presentation of his research at the academy was inspiring.
(C) Due to a lack of funds, the project had been put on hold.
(D) The student retention rate has increased over the last several years.

141. (A) reserved
(B) revised
(C) existing
(D) temporary

142. (A) in spite of
(B) due to
(C) depending upon
(D) across from

GO ON TO THE NEXT PAGE

Questions 143-146 refer to the following instructions.

Packing Shipments: How to Prepare Fragile Merchandise

Despite making our best effort to avoid damage to items loaded on our trucks, we are unable to compensate for breakage of fragile merchandise. -------, it is very important
143.
to make sure that all items are appropriately packed to avoid losses. Reused packaging material loses its ------- strength and may not provide adequate cushioning. If you have
144.
to reuse an old box, for example, inspect it carefully for any damage or irregular surfaces. ------- may result in the box tearing or changing shape during transit, increasing the risk of
145.
damage to your items. It is especially important to keep items separate from each other as well. -------. That way, they will be much less likely to collide with each other and break while
146.
being loaded, transported, and unloaded.

143. (A) Regardless
(B) Therefore
(C) However
(D) Finally

144. (A) subjective
(B) famous
(C) original
(D) innovative

145. (A) These
(B) Neither
(C) Others
(D) Few

146. (A) We strongly recommend against this method.
(B) You are welcome to send them via e-mail.
(C) As an alternative, you may purchase damage insurance for your merchandise.
(D) For this purpose, wrap the items well and allow enough space between them.

PART 7

Directions: In this part you will read a selection of texts, such as magazine and newspaper articles, e-mails, and instant messages. Each text or set of texts is followed by several questions. Select the best answer for each question and mark the letter (A), (B), (C), or (D) on your answer sheet.

Questions 147-148 refer to the following information.

http://www.e-heaven.com

Notice to Marbletech Tablet Users:

Marbletech's latest tablet PC will be released on August 1. This product is already available for preorder at Electronic Heaven's Web site, www.e-heaven.com, or from Marbletech's Web site, www.marbletech.com/tablets.

And for a limited time only, you can win a pair of Marbletech headphones. To secure an opportunity to win, just email the serial number on the back of the user guide to contest@marbletech.com. Fifty winners will be notified on October 1.

147. What will happen on August 1?

(A) A computer course will be offered.
(B) A promotion will end.
(C) A device will be launched.
(D) A prize will be given.

148. How can a contest be entered?

(A) By spending a certain amount
(B) By sending a number
(C) By providing some feedback
(D) By attending an event

Questions 149-150 refer to the following e-mail.

From	Eva Vasquez
To	All employees
Date	21 January
Subject	New process

This is to inform all employees of Berkins Adventure Tours that we will no longer be keeping paper records of customers who sign up for our adventure tours. You will now enter customer information into our new computer database.

During last week's training session, a staff member asked if we could provide a data entry sample (as shown below). This new system will save us time and help us to better monitor which tours are doing well.

Berkins Adventure Tours

Last name, First name
Hong, Erica

Address line 1 [company building name, housing complex, number]
Heureux Apt. #2019

Address line 2 [building number, road name]
112 Royal Street

City, State Zip Code
New Orleans, LA 70116

(Area code) Phone number
(504) 555-6519

Tour code: 3894
Amount: $450

Thank you for your cooperation in this matter. Please let me know if you have any questions.

Eva Vasquez
Berkins Adventure Tours

149. What did the company recently change?

(A) How to order supplies
(B) How to train staff
(C) How to advertise tours
(D) How to store data

150. Who is Ms. Hong?

(A) A product designer
(B) A computer programmer
(C) An adventure tourist
(D) A travel agent

Questions 151-152 refer to the following memo.

To: Employees at Bowman, Inc.
From: Office manager
Date: August 1
Subject: Printing supplies

Starting today, each department will need to pay a small fee for paper supplies taken from the supply closet. For every ream of printer paper your team takes, please have someone leave 75 cents. Be aware that this cost is still well below the retail price you would pay at your local store.

Whenever you need more paper, just put your money in the labeled jar by the closet door. As always, we will purchase the best quality printer paper and restock it every other week. On behalf of the company, thank you for your understanding. We will do our best to make sure that paper is always readily available to our staff members.

151. What is the purpose of the memo?

(A) To clarify a misunderstanding
(B) To describe new products
(C) To announce a new policy
(D) To explain a printing process

152. What are employees asked to do?

(A) Keep the supply closet clean
(B) Purchase their own paper
(C) Submit monthly order forms
(D) Place money into a container

Questions 153-154 refer to the following text message chain.

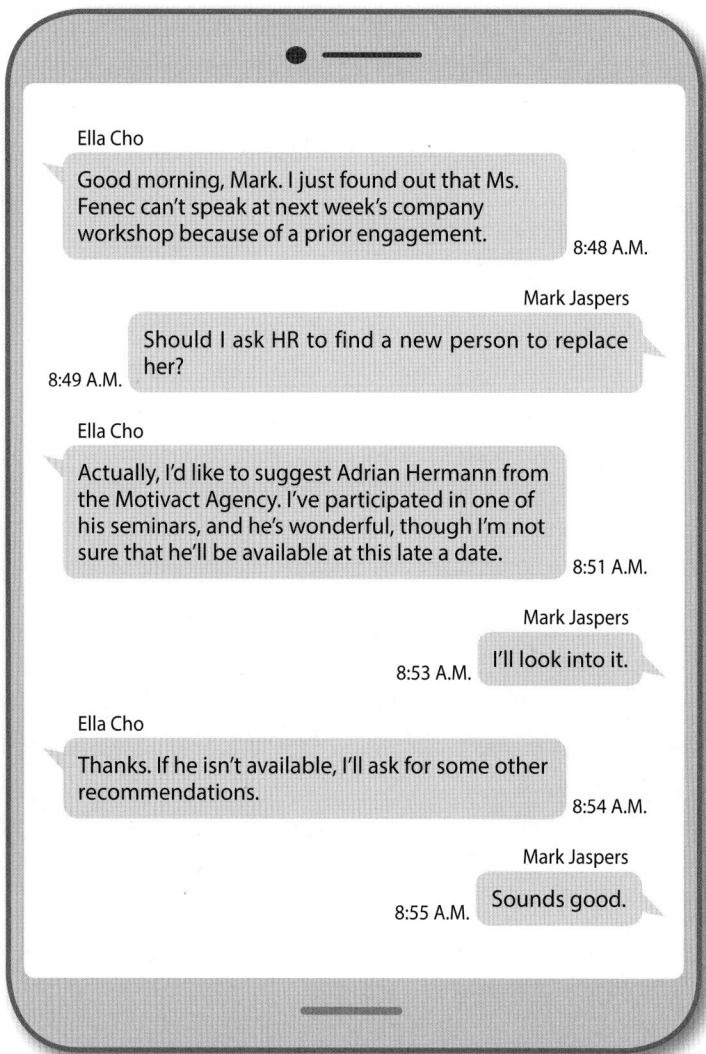

153. Why did Ms. Cho contact Mr. Jaspers?

(A) To change a scheduled activity
(B) To request a document
(C) To announce a cancellation
(D) To discuss a new venue location

154. At 8:53 A.M., what does Mr. Jaspers mean when he writes, "I'll look into it"?

(A) He will find out about Mr. Hermann's availability.
(B) He will learn more about the Motivact Agency.
(C) He will ask about changing the dates for a retreat.
(D) He will schedule a meeting with the HR manager.

Questions 155-157 refer to the following notice.

Rock Creek Arts Drive

The Rock Creek Arts Drive will be held from 7:30 A.M. to 7:30 P.M. on the first Saturday of the month, June 3. We would greatly appreciate donations from the public before the event. All art donations can be dropped off at the site of the drive, in front of the auditorium of Rock Creek High School, or at the Parks and Recreation office located at 1022 E. Loyola Drive. Items will be accepted through June 2.

Profits from the drive will be used for a new classroom building at Rock Creek High School and for the Arts After School initiative, set up by Nora Lanta, which received a National Teachers' Award for its creativity.

We will need help on the day of the drive. If you are interested in volunteering to organize items, help with ticket sales, or clean up afterward, call Marylou Ferris at 555-5296. You're also welcome just to show up to lend a hand on June 3, at 7:30 A.M.

155. Where will the arts drive take place?

(A) At a government office
(B) At a park
(C) At a museum
(D) At a local school

156. According to the notice, how will some of the money from the sales be used?

(A) To fund a new park
(B) To help an educational program
(C) To rebuild a damaged structure
(D) To hire more city employees

157. Who most likely is Ms. Ferris?

(A) An art instructor
(B) A community event organizer
(C) The painter of a mural
(D) The president of an association

Questions 158-160 refer to the following e-mail.

To	l.campbell@rvacorporation.co.ca
From	sgrendal@globalea.org
Date	March 1
Subject	Information

Ms. Campbell,

We appreciate your loyal membership to the Global Engineering Association. I would like to let you know that the advance registration for this year's convention in Bogota will end on May 31. —[1]—. This time around, the convention will have more than 200 exhibitors, include product demos, and feature famous speakers. —[2]—.

Advance registration lets you save $55 off the regular price. —[3]—. You will also get first priority for the welcome luncheon and an exclusive tour of the historic district at the heart of the city. Please go to our Web site to sign up. —[4]—. However, if you would like to register over the phone, please call (+57) 1-555-7575. Make sure to have your membership information handy.

Best regards,

Stephen Grendal
Membership Accounts Manager

---

158. What most likely is Ms. Campbell's occupation?

(A) Accountant
(B) Event planner
(C) Engineer
(D) Tour guide

159. What is NOT a stated benefit of advance registration for the convention?

(A) An upgraded flight seat
(B) A tour of Bogota
(C) Entry to a special meal
(D) Discounted registration costs

160. In which of the positions marked [1], [2], [3], and [4] does the following sentence best belong?

"There, you can also view a detailed schedule of the convention."

(A) [1]
(B) [2]
(C) [3]
(D) [4]

Questions 161-163 refer to the following contract.

Evanscamp Auto Repair and Maintenance Contract Renewal
Your loyalty as a customer is appreciated!

Name: Tiara Graves
Address: 75 Albert Street, Cedar Vale, Queensland, Australia
Postal Code: 4285
Phone Number: 07-5550-2509

Signature: *Tiara Graves*
Amount to be Paid: $250

Basic Package: $250
This plan is good for one year and provides basic care for your vehicle.
Benefits include:
- Oil changes
- Transmission fluid checks
- Tire rotations
- Air filter inspections
- Drive belt checks

Premium Package: $425
This plan provides car owners with two years of hassle-free care. In addition to the basic maintenance of your vehicle, it includes 24-hour service and roadside assistance for free.

Inspection: All maintenance inspections must be scheduled during regular business hours, Monday through Friday, from 9 A.M. to 6 P.M.

Service Calls: A charge of $75 will be made to the customer's account when a service call is placed after business hours or on weekends. However, this fee is waived for Premium Package members.

---

161. What is implied about Ms. Graves?

(A) She is training to become a mechanic.
(B) She will purchase a new vehicle.
(C) She would like to upgrade her membership.
(D) She has entered a contract with Evanscamp before.

162. What is NOT part of the Basic Package?

(A) Checking the filtration system
(B) Washing the car
(C) Examining the drive belts
(D) Replacing the oil

163. What additional benefit is included in the price of the Premium Package?

(A) Servicing beyond normal operating hours
(B) Maintenance work twice a year
(C) Complimentary auto parts
(D) Insurance for accidents

GO ON TO THE NEXT PAGE

Questions 164-167 refer to the following online chat discussion.

Wendy Rosella [9:03 A.M.]
Cory and I are going to grab something to eat at about noon. Would anyone like to come with us?

Blake Eaton [9:04 A.M.]
I might be able to, but I need to finish the monthly financial report first. Where will you go?

Wendy Rosella [9:05 A.M.]
Well, we are considering trying the new Vietnamese place at 4th Avenue: Ho Chi Max.

Fabiana Peron [9:06 A.M.]
You're going to be disappointed, then, because they closed for good last week.

Wendy Rosella [9:07 A.M.]
What a pity. I read great reviews about it.

Fabiana Peron [9:08 A.M.]
What about Rodeo Phở across the street? They have special deals on Tuesdays.

Wendy Rosella [9:09 A.M.]
That's a good idea. Is everyone else OK with Rodeo Phở?

Blake Eaton [9:10 A.M.]
Sure, but I'll probably get there around 12:20.

Cory Smith [9:11 A.M.]
That should be fine. Also, Blake, I just sent you an attachment with the Sales Department's expenditures.

164. What are the writers discussing?

(A) Where to have lunch
(B) Where to hold a corporate picnic
(C) Which menu is the cheapest
(D) Which restaurant has the best service

165. What information does Ms. Peron provide about Ho Chi Max?

(A) Her friend has been there before.
(B) Dishes there have small portions.
(C) It went out of business.
(D) It opens later on Tuesdays.

166. At 9:07 A.M., why most likely does Ms. Rosella write, "What a pity"?

(A) She already has an appointment.
(B) An eatery is inconveniently located.
(C) She was unable to visit a restaurant.
(D) Ms. Peron will not finish on time.

167. What does Mr. Eaton decide to do?

(A) Complete an assignment tomorrow
(B) Eat some food with his colleagues
(C) Look up different restaurants
(D) Arrange a meal delivery service

GO ON TO THE NEXT PAGE

Questions 168-171 refer to the following article.

SOR, Inc. Earns Praise

Lenexa (August 10) – SOR, Inc. has kept its promise to purchase at least 65 percent of its products from small farms. This promise was made when the firm decided to join the Sustainable Sourcing Project created by local activists. The company specializes in supplying coffee and tea to restaurants and other retail clients in the country.

One of the conditions of taking part in the project has been to interact directly with the growers of agricultural products to assist in the community development at the production sites. As a result, this Kansas-based company has invested over $5 million in schools and health clinics in five states.

"We are very excited," said SOR President Leon Madrigal. "When we joined the project five years ago, a lot of people thought it would damage our business. But we knew it was the right way. Supporting the communities that supply our products is our duty as a responsible partner, and it's very important to us."

In addition to participating in the ethical sourcing project, SOR is planning to launch a fundraiser focused on women's health education in their grower communities. To learn more about this initiative, check out their Web site: www.sorjavatraders.com.

SOR, Inc. employs 200 staff at its Lenexa headquarters and currently supplies more than 500 retail clients.

168. What is the main subject of the article?

(A) SOR, Inc. acquires its products from countries all over the world.
(B) SOR, Inc. is planning to add wholesale distribution to its services.
(C) SOR, Inc. provides health care and education services for its employees.
(D) SOR, Inc. is dedicated to benefiting communities that supply its products.

169. What type of business is SOR, Inc.?

(A) A manufacturer of hospital appliances
(B) A supplier of restaurant utensils
(C) An importer of farm equipment
(D) A distributor of beverage products

170. The word "conditions" in paragraph 2, line 1, is closest in meaning to

(A) situations
(B) positions
(C) terms
(D) forms

171. What is stated about the Sustainable Sourcing Project?

(A) It generated over $5 million in revenue.
(B) It requires contact with farmers.
(C) It has created several hundred new jobs.
(D) Its members are mainly located in Kansas.

Questions 172-175 refer to the following article.

Alamar's Plans for Trade Show

Edinburgh (9 May) - Western Europe's largest jewelry retailer, Alamar Accessories, announced today that it would not be displaying this year's collection at the Edinburgh Jewelry Trade Show this June. —[1]—.

The show has traditionally been considered a substantial source of publicity in the jewelry business, with the world's most prestigious retailers competing to present their brands in unique ways. It continues to draw media attention and celebrity participation. Recent studies, however, have found that the average consumer has little interest in such events. —[2]—.

In a recent interview at Alamar's main office in Amsterdam, CEO Sanaa Ayoub explained that her company would still participate very actively in the show, despite the decision not to formally present their collection. —[3]—. "Even though we won't be participating in that portion of the event, the Alamar team will be there for a number of meetings with our various business partners," she explained. "But to share this year's collection with our target market, we'll be showcasing our latest product lines on www.AlamarEU.com for the duration of the trade show."

As to why the company has chosen this unusual strategy, Ms. Ayoub explained that Alamar's objective was to create interest in new designs by showing samples to consumers who already knew and liked the brand. Also, by presenting their collection separately, Alamar will avoid clients comparing their offerings side-by-side with those of their rivals. "We believe our collection has everything a customer needs, so there's no need to look elsewhere," Ayoub added. —[4]—.

---

172. In the article, the word "substantial" in paragraph 2, line 2, is closest in meaning to

(A) generous
(B) heavy
(C) wholesome
(D) major

173. According to the article, what will Alamar Accessories do during the trade show?

(A) Make a joint presentation with a business partner
(B) Provide information on a Web site
(C) Show a new television commercial
(D) Hold a press conference for reporters

174. What is one reason stated for Alamar Accessories changing its trade show plans?

(A) It hopes to focus on improving its collection.
(B) It believes the trade show creates a negative impression.
(C) It wants to avoid being compared with rivals.
(D) It needs to reserve all available times for meetings.

175. In which of the positions marked [1], [2], [3], and [4] does the following sentence best belong?

"Therefore, Alamar's announcement did not surprise industry analysts."

(A) [1]
(B) [2]
(C) [3]
(D) [4]

GO ON TO THE NEXT PAGE

Questions 176-180 refer to the following e-mail and chart.

To: Michelle Liu, Accounting Director
From: Victor Gomez, Marketing Manager
Date: December 5
Subject: Budget Proposal
Attachment: marketing_budget

Dear Ms. Liu,

Attached is the Marketing Department's budget proposal for the upcoming year. Please review it at your earliest convenience. You will see that we can cut costs in some categories. I mainly looked for ways to reduce expenses in the advertising budget (our largest expense category). I believe we can lower costs by discontinuing print media ads starting from the 2nd quarter. However, the CEO wants to increase promotional resources for our end-of-the-year sale by 20 percent, approximately $5,000. This basically offsets the savings from that category. As a result, our budget will remain the same as last year's.

Please let me know if you have any questions about the proposal. I have interviews lined up until Thursday, but I will make room in my schedule if you would like to meet.

Best regards,

Victor Gomez
Marketing Manager

Marketing Department Budget
Victor Gomez

	1st Quarter	2nd Quarter	3rd Quarter	4th Quarter	Total
Staff Workshops	$5,000	$0	$0	$0	$5,000
Product Promotion & Advertising	$6,000	$2,000	$4,000	$8,000	$20,000
Market Research	$1,500	$2,500	$1,000	$1,500	$6,500
Business Travel	$3,000	$4,500	$7,000	$5,000	$19,500
Total	$15,500	$9,000	$12,000	$14,500	$51,000

176. What is the purpose of the e-mail?

(A) To obtain approval for a financial plan
(B) To summarize points of a conference
(C) To discuss the details of a marketing class
(D) To apologize for an accounting mistake

177. According to Mr. Gomez, how much did his department spend in total on promotion and advertising last year?

(A) $5,000
(B) $15,000
(C) $20,000
(D) $46,500

178. What does Mr. Gomez plan to do next year?

(A) Stop using print media
(B) Transfer to another branch
(C) Hire more employees
(D) Teach advertising at a university

179. What is one kind of expense that is likely included in the chart?

(A) Flight tickets
(B) Staff wages
(C) New equipment
(D) Employee recruitment

180. What does the chart indicate about Mr. Gomez's department?

(A) It is investing in more digital ads this year.
(B) It hosts workshops at the beginning of the year.
(C) It will have a larger budget than last year.
(D) It is hiring a new director soon.

Questions 181-185 refer to the following article and letter.

Community Observer
by Kareena Sinha, Staff Reporter

Lawston (April 2) — Nearly a year's worth of renovations wrapped up last Wednesday, allowing the public to finally set foot inside Lawston's updated civic center. For employees, it was business as usual at this cultural and commercial landmark.

General manager David Estes couldn't be happier to be back in the civic center after spending many months in a nearby municipal building. "It took several weeks to get everything set up here," he explained. "Actually, compared to the delays we had to endure, moving in was probably the easiest part of the renovation process. And we're so pleased to be in such an attractive building."

Visitors also had positive things to say. The central lobby's large windows let in the bright spring sunlight, making the space appear spacious and cheerful. Eva Martinez, engineer and Pebbleton resident, said, "I was curious to see how the renovated facility looked. This is the only civic center in the southern part of the state, so the renovations were necessary. But I didn't expect it to also look so nice."

Part of the project involved adding some new features. There was some controversy about erecting a large fountain in the main lobby of the east building. The cost of creating the fountain exceeded the initial estimate and was the subject of many town hall meetings. However, the feature that stands out the most is the creation of an art gallery that showcases work by some of Lawston's famous artists. Daria Forde, Lawston city planner, said, "We wanted a tourist spot to show visitors our artistic past alongside contemporary cultural events."

Editor's Mailbox

To the Editor:

I felt that the article in the April 2 edition was incomplete without the acknowledgement of the business partners who made the civic center renovations a reality. There was not a single sentence about Jason Doiron, whose generous donation covered nearly all of the construction costs.

Overall, while the article summed up the sense of pride we all feel in this city improvement, it did not bring up the serious traffic situation now faced by this part of town. And it's only going to get worse. The civic center also now houses a new tourist attraction, which I believe was a costly and wasteful addition. That's why I'm going to petition Lawston's city planner to make roadway changes on Monday, April 29.

Sincerely,

Eric Conrad

181. What is the purpose of the article?

(A) To request additional funds for restoration work
(B) To promote tours of a new facility
(C) To publicize the reopening of a building
(D) To describe a structure's history

182. What is mentioned about the civic center project?

(A) It took less than a year.
(B) It required the construction of several new buildings.
(C) It was supported by famous artists.
(D) It was finished on time.

183. What does Mr. Conrad indicate was missing from the article?

(A) An indication of the public's views on the project
(B) The date of a groundbreaking ceremony
(C) The location of additional parking lots
(D) A mention of some project contributors

184. What opinion about the renovation project does Mr. Conrad express?

(A) He feels the project should have been delayed.
(B) He thinks the art gallery should not have been constructed.
(C) He believes that the project should have been completed earlier.
(D) He wants a wider variety of art to be on display.

185. Who will Mr. Conrad meet on Monday?

(A) Mr. Estes
(B) Ms. Martinez
(C) Ms. Forde
(D) Mr. Doiron

Questions 186-190 refer to the following article, product label, and review.

Changes in Store for Napleese

NAPLES (October 27) — The familiar family-owned Napleese line of cheeses may soon get an update.

After nearly nine months of intense bidding, North American company OnFood Corporation purchased the struggling Italian cheese manufacturer. OnFood plans to expand distribution of the beloved brand to overseas markets. This may involve changing the packaging to have a more modern design.

Tens of thousands of kilos of Napleese cheeses are purchased every month. Sold in packages picturing a cow dressed in an ancient Roman costume underneath the words, "Empire of Cheese," the much-loved cheeses are known and trusted by consumers across Italy for their excellent flavor. Despite this, OnFood does plan to make changes.

"Much of Napleese's charm will remain," said OnFood Corporation's International Marketing Director, Blane Sapore. "However, the cheeses will become products recognizable as part of the OnFood's line of goods. The shape of the containers, the slogan, and even the name of the product are all being discussed."

Cheese lovers across Italy are concerned that the quality of the cheeses will be the biggest of the changes, with a loss of both its character and its good taste. OnFood has stated on numerous occasions that Napleese's cheese-making processes will remain untouched and that organic dairy products will continue to be used.

Napleese Cheese
An Original Italian Product from Naples

350g Cumin and Paprika Parmesan

Produced by Napleese, an OnFood Corporation brand, Detroit, MI

Try our other customer favorites:
Sage-rubbed Mozzarella
Poppy Seed Swiss

Look for our winter exclusive:
Crushed Mint Brie
Available Soon!

http://www.napleese.it/feedback

I moved to the United States from a small village near Naples this year to attend university, and it was a delight to see Napleese in local supermarkets. I bought all of the different types of cheeses and found them to be quite similar to how they taste back home. In particular, the mozzarella is worthy of praise. I'm looking forward to trying the special winter item.

I do have some criticism for the limited choices offered here in the U.S. Why aren't all of Napleese's cheeses offered? While you can find juniper-smoked edam, where is the grape leaf feta? I especially miss my favorite, cinnamon curry gorgonzola. Although Napleese-brand cheeses are somewhat more expensive here, they are far superior to other kinds of cheese. I'm happy to pay the additional cost for such a wonderful taste of home.

Lisa Rossi

January 21

186. What is the purpose of the article?

(A) To advertise a new line of cheeses
(B) To report on a corporate transaction
(C) To discuss new production methods
(D) To compare different management styles

187. What change to Napleese's cheese is reflected on the product label?

(A) The package size
(B) The ingredient list
(C) The company slogan
(D) The product name

188. What is indicated about Ms. Rossi?

(A) She has a part-time job at a supermarket.
(B) She has been to Napleese's plant.
(C) She relocated to a different country recently.
(D) She prefers Swiss to other types of cheese.

189. According to the review, what is Ms. Rossi dissatisfied about?

(A) She is not able to buy her favorite kind of cheese.
(B) Cheese in the United States is more expensive than in Italy.
(C) She is unable to locate Napleese cheeses in her area.
(D) Napleese cheeses are no longer high-quality products.

190. What flavor is Ms. Rossi excited to try?

(A) Cumin and paprika parmesan
(B) Juniper-smoked edam
(C) Cinnamon curry gorgonzola
(D) Crushed mint brie

GO ON TO THE NEXT PAGE

Questions 191-195 refer to the following e-mails and meeting minutes.

To	: Nadine Ortiz
From	: Seth Lindt
Date	: Thursday, May 14
Subject	: Meeting guidelines
Attachment	: handouts.doc, schedule.rtf

Dear Nadine,

I really appreciate your offer to take notes at tomorrow's meeting of the board. Since this will be your first time covering an executive event, I wanted to go over the following guidelines with you.

Please take note of the executives and department heads present, as well as any who are not in attendance. We publish board meeting notes on our investor relations Web page, but be sure to email the notes and reports to those unable to attend. I have attached my budget report for tomorrow, so please include it when you send the notes. I also included the agenda for your reference.

Many different departments will be under review, but you only need to convey the most important information. Be sure that your notes are concise so that investors can reference them quickly. Utilizing bullet points and shortening department names will be helpful in that regard. Note that it is normal to refer to staff and executives by their last names.

If there is anything you want to specifically discuss, please get in touch. Good luck!

Seth

Board Meeting Minutes
Friday, May 15
10:00 A.M. – 12:00 P.M.

Present: Jennifer Ruiz, Nathan Weiss, Carol Hassan, Yvonne Lim, Wes Cooper, Ali Flynn, Dana Nguyen, Anish Adjala, and all board members

Absent: Wendy Wodja, Allan Smith

- Flynn and Nguyen were in charge of Marketing's product announcement event at the DigiWorld Conference in Santa Fe in early March. They will be attending again next year in Dallas because we got a lot of positive feedback from this year's event.

- Cooper explained that A/R employees have successfully transitioned to a new computer system. Although several problems occurred during the transition, Hald in IT was able to deal with them.

- Yvonne mentioned that the customer help desk is very busy, and for this reason, she requested an increased operating budget to hire some new workers.

- This year's corporate retreat will be held at La Petite Cerise Resort on Saturday, November 13. However, since Weiss from Accounting is going to be recruiting in San Palomar that week, Wes will take over the arrangements.

Minutes compiled by Nadine Ortiz

To	Nadine Ortiz
From	Wendy Wodja
Date	Monday, May 18
Subject	Board meeting minutes

Dear Ms. Ortiz,

Great work on your first time taking notes for the board meeting. I found them to be quite useful as I was unable to attend on Friday. The format was certainly easy to read through.

I have a couple of corrections to point out. First of all, Jennifer Ruiz was also in attendance at the DigiWorld Conference. She is planning to attend next year's event as well. Also, it might be a better idea to write out the names of the various departments you mention. Outside investors often visit our Web site, and some might not be aware that A/R refers to Accounts Receivable, for example.

Once again, thanks for all your help.

Wendy Wodja

---

191. What is suggested about Mr. Lindt?

(A) He will provide a report of the board meeting.
(B) He will not attend the board meeting.
(C) He will go on a business trip to Dallas.
(D) He will add a schedule to a Web page.

192. In the first e-mail, the word "convey" in paragraph 3, line 1, is closest in meaning to

(A) bring
(B) transport
(C) express
(D) allow

193. What is Mr. Weiss usually in charge of?

(A) Taking notes during a monthly event
(B) Organizing a yearly corporate event
(C) Fixing computer software problems
(D) Solving company staffing issues

194. What did Ms. Ruiz do recently?

(A) Demonstrated a product
(B) Negotiated a business contract
(C) Traveled to Santa Fe
(D) Transferred to the IT team

195. What recommendation for taking meeting notes do Mr. Lindt and Ms. Wodja disagree on?

(A) Checking who is present
(B) Making an agenda
(C) Shortening department names
(D) Using participant's last names

GO ON TO THE NEXT PAGE

Questions 196-200 refer to the following notice, Web page, and invoice.

New Zealand Industry Association (NZIA)

The NZIA is pleased to recognize the recipient of this year's National Excellence Award. Since beginning his career 40 years ago, director Francis Reid has been dedicated to teaching history through film. Please join us in honoring Mr. Reid on 8 November at 6:30 P.M. in the Grand Hall at the Rubar Resort in Auckland. A world-famous ballet group, The Flying Swans, will showcase their talents right after the ceremony.

Many of Francis Reid's movies have helped us develop a deeper understanding and respect for the country we live in. His first breakthrough film, *Kiwis on Wheels*, discusses the impact of vehicles in the early 1900s and how the steady growth of cars affected our economy over time. *Through the Trails*, his best movie to date, documents one local family's struggle under the rule of the British Empire in the 1800s. And currently under production in collaboration with artist Nicole Whittle, the film, *Painting the Country*, recounts the first days of Wellington.

Please go to www.nzia.co.nz to sign up for the event. The Rubar Resort will offer special room discounts to event participants. For additional details, check out www.rubarresort.co.nz/nzia.

www.rubarresort.co.nz/nzia

Featured Event

New Zealand Industry Association
20th Annual Awards Ceremony

Hurry and book your room for this special occasion on 8 November. Event guests can reserve rooms at a special discount from 7 November to 9 November; included in this reduced rate are a three-course meal and live entertainment at the ceremony. Please call us at +64 9-363-5555 for complete information about room types and detailed pricing.

If you make your reservation through our latest mobile application, you can earn 1,500 points towards your Rubar Resort Rewards Membership. This application enables customers to easily find and book a room on any smart device. This deal expires on 30 November and is only offered to current or new members of the Rubar Resort Rewards Program.

Rubar Resort (Auckland)

Invoice Date: 10 November
Guest Name: Jennifer Davis
Room No.: 819
Phone Number: (342)-552-2300
Check-in Date: 8 November
Check-out Date: 9 November
Rubar Resort Rewards Member No.: 1240982
Membership points: 1,500 (promotional bonus)
Amount: $110 per night (NZIA price)
Tax: 10% ($11)
TOTAL: $121.00
Credit card: (last four digits: 7788)

Thank you for staying with us!

196. What is featured in all of Mr. Reid's listed films?

(A) Reviews of different vehicles
(B) A plot with a mountain setting
(C) Paintings by Nicole Whittle
(D) An emphasis on New Zealand's history

197. In the notice, the word "recounts" in paragraph 2, line 6, is closest in meaning to

(A) describes
(B) calculates
(C) relates
(D) duplicates

198. What is indicated about the special room discount?

(A) It can be applied with other promotional discounts.
(B) It can only be used by rewards program members.
(C) It is available for a limited time.
(D) It is only offered to Auckland residents.

199. What is included in the price of a room reserved for the awards ceremony?

(A) A speech by a famous director
(B) A dance show
(C) A breakfast buffet
(D) Entry to a painting exhibit

200. What is implied about Ms. Davis?

(A) She used the resort's mobile application.
(B) Her membership program application was rejected.
(C) She will book another room on November 30.
(D) Her credit card was not processed correctly.

Stop! This is the end of the test. If you finish before time is called, you may go back to Part 5, 6, and 7 and check your work.

NO TEST MATERIAL ON THIS PAGE

NO TEST MATERIAL ON THIS PAGE

Answer Keys

MP3, 해석, 해설 온라인 무료 제공
모바일: QR코드 스캔을 통해 MP3 음원 바로 듣기 / 정답, 해석, 해설 바로 보기
PC: 파고다북스 사이트(www.pagodabook.com) 접속 / 로그인 후 다운로드

Listening Comprehension

1 (B)	2 (C)	3 (B)	4 (C)	5 (C)
6 (C)	7 (A)	8 (A)	9 (C)	10 (C)
11 (B)	12 (A)	13 (A)	14 (A)	15 (C)
16 (A)	17 (C)	18 (B)	19 (A)	20 (B)
21 (B)	22 (C)	23 (A)	24 (A)	25 (C)
26 (B)	27 (C)	28 (A)	29 (A)	30 (C)
31 (B)	32 (C)	33 (A)	34 (C)	35 (D)
36 (D)	37 (A)	38 (D)	39 (B)	40 (C)
41 (D)	42 (A)	43 (A)	44 (B)	45 (A)
46 (C)	47 (D)	48 (A)	49 (A)	50 (D)
51 (A)	52 (A)	53 (D)	54 (A)	55 (C)
56 (A)	57 (D)	58 (C)	59 (A)	60 (A)
61 (B)	62 (A)	63 (D)	64 (B)	65 (C)
66 (C)	67 (D)	68 (D)	69 (C)	70 (C)
71 (C)	72 (B)	73 (D)	74 (D)	75 (B)
76 (D)	77 (D)	78 (C)	79 (B)	80 (B)
81 (D)	82 (A)	83 (C)	84 (D)	85 (B)
86 (D)	87 (A)	88 (A)	89 (C)	90 (A)
91 (C)	92 (B)	93 (C)	94 (D)	95 (A)
96 (B)	97 (D)	98 (A)	99 (A)	100 (B)

Reading Comprehension

101 (A)	102 (D)	103 (C)	104 (B)	105 (D)
106 (A)	107 (B)	108 (D)	109 (A)	110 (C)
111 (B)	112 (C)	113 (A)	114 (A)	115 (C)
116 (A)	117 (C)	118 (C)	119 (D)	120 (B)
121 (A)	122 (D)	123 (A)	124 (C)	125 (C)
126 (A)	127 (A)	128 (A)	129 (D)	130 (B)
131 (C)	132 (D)	133 (A)	134 (D)	135 (A)
136 (B)	137 (D)	138 (D)	139 (A)	140 (C)
141 (C)	142 (D)	143 (B)	144 (C)	145 (A)
146 (D)	147 (C)	148 (B)	149 (D)	150 (C)
151 (C)	152 (D)	153 (C)	154 (A)	155 (D)
156 (B)	157 (B)	158 (C)	159 (A)	160 (D)
161 (D)	162 (B)	163 (A)	164 (A)	165 (C)
166 (C)	167 (B)	168 (D)	169 (D)	170 (C)
171 (B)	172 (D)	173 (B)	174 (C)	175 (B)
176 (A)	177 (C)	178 (A)	179 (A)	180 (B)
181 (C)	182 (A)	183 (D)	184 (B)	185 (C)
186 (B)	187 (C)	188 (C)	189 (A)	190 (D)
191 (A)	192 (C)	193 (B)	194 (C)	195 (C)
196 (D)	197 (A)	198 (C)	199 (B)	200 (A)

파고다토익 Vol.2 시험 직전 마무리 모의고사 TEST 3

초판 1쇄 인쇄 2018년 7월 4일
초판 1쇄 발행 2018년 7월 4일
초판 11쇄 발행 2024년 9월 30일

지 은 이 | 파고다교육그룹 언어교육연구소
펴 낸 이 | 박경실
펴 낸 곳 | PAGODA Books 파고다북스
출판등록 | 2005년 5월 27일 제 300-2005-90호
주   소 | 06614 서울특별시 서초구 강남대로 419, 19층(서초동, 파고다타워)
전   화 | (02) 6940-4070
팩   스 | (02) 536-0660
홈페이지 | www.pagodabook.com

저작권자 | ⓒ 2018 파고다아카데미

이 책의 저작권은 저자와 출판사에 있습니다. 서면에 의한 저작권자와 출판사의 허락 없이
내용의 일부 혹은 전부를 인용 및 복제하거나 발췌하는 것을 금합니다.

Copyright ⓒ 2018 by PAGODA Academy

All rights reserved. No part of this publication may be reproduced, stored
in a retrieval system, or transmitted, in any form, or by any means, electronic,
mechanical, photocopying, recording or otherwise, without the prior written
permission of the copyright holder and the publisher.

ISBN 978-89-6281-817-8 (13740)

파고다북스   www.pagodabook.com
파고다 어학원   www.pagoda21.com
파고다 인강   www.pagodastar.com
테스트 클리닉   www.testclinic.com

▎낙장 및 파본은 구매처에서 교환해 드립니다.

PAGODA Books

PAGODA Books

DATA SHEET

※ 본 OMR 카드는 실전 연습용으로 제공되고 있으며, OMR 성적 처리는 별도로 제공되지 않음을 알려드립니다.

ANSWER SHEET

PAGODA Books

문제번호

성명

LISTENING COMPREHENSION (Part I ~ IV)

NO.	ANSWER A B C D	NO.	ANSWER A B C D	NO.	ANSWER A B C D	NO.	ANSWER A B C D	NO.	ANSWER A B C D
1	Ⓐ Ⓑ Ⓒ Ⓓ	21	Ⓐ Ⓑ Ⓒ Ⓓ	41	Ⓐ Ⓑ Ⓒ Ⓓ	61	Ⓐ Ⓑ Ⓒ Ⓓ	81	Ⓐ Ⓑ Ⓒ Ⓓ
2	Ⓐ Ⓑ Ⓒ Ⓓ	22	Ⓐ Ⓑ Ⓒ Ⓓ	42	Ⓐ Ⓑ Ⓒ Ⓓ	62	Ⓐ Ⓑ Ⓒ Ⓓ	82	Ⓐ Ⓑ Ⓒ Ⓓ
3	Ⓐ Ⓑ Ⓒ Ⓓ	23	Ⓐ Ⓑ Ⓒ Ⓓ	43	Ⓐ Ⓑ Ⓒ Ⓓ	63	Ⓐ Ⓑ Ⓒ Ⓓ	83	Ⓐ Ⓑ Ⓒ Ⓓ
4	Ⓐ Ⓑ Ⓒ Ⓓ	24	Ⓐ Ⓑ Ⓒ Ⓓ	44	Ⓐ Ⓑ Ⓒ Ⓓ	64	Ⓐ Ⓑ Ⓒ Ⓓ	84	Ⓐ Ⓑ Ⓒ Ⓓ
5	Ⓐ Ⓑ Ⓒ Ⓓ	25	Ⓐ Ⓑ Ⓒ Ⓓ	45	Ⓐ Ⓑ Ⓒ Ⓓ	65	Ⓐ Ⓑ Ⓒ Ⓓ	85	Ⓐ Ⓑ Ⓒ Ⓓ
6	Ⓐ Ⓑ Ⓒ Ⓓ	26	Ⓐ Ⓑ Ⓒ Ⓓ	46	Ⓐ Ⓑ Ⓒ Ⓓ	66	Ⓐ Ⓑ Ⓒ Ⓓ	86	Ⓐ Ⓑ Ⓒ Ⓓ
7	Ⓐ Ⓑ Ⓒ Ⓓ	27	Ⓐ Ⓑ Ⓒ Ⓓ	47	Ⓐ Ⓑ Ⓒ Ⓓ	67	Ⓐ Ⓑ Ⓒ Ⓓ	87	Ⓐ Ⓑ Ⓒ Ⓓ
8	Ⓐ Ⓑ Ⓒ Ⓓ	28	Ⓐ Ⓑ Ⓒ Ⓓ	48	Ⓐ Ⓑ Ⓒ Ⓓ	68	Ⓐ Ⓑ Ⓒ Ⓓ	88	Ⓐ Ⓑ Ⓒ Ⓓ
9	Ⓐ Ⓑ Ⓒ Ⓓ	29	Ⓐ Ⓑ Ⓒ Ⓓ	49	Ⓐ Ⓑ Ⓒ Ⓓ	69	Ⓐ Ⓑ Ⓒ Ⓓ	89	Ⓐ Ⓑ Ⓒ Ⓓ
10	Ⓐ Ⓑ Ⓒ Ⓓ	30	Ⓐ Ⓑ Ⓒ Ⓓ	50	Ⓐ Ⓑ Ⓒ Ⓓ	70	Ⓐ Ⓑ Ⓒ Ⓓ	90	Ⓐ Ⓑ Ⓒ Ⓓ
11	Ⓐ Ⓑ Ⓒ Ⓓ	31	Ⓐ Ⓑ Ⓒ Ⓓ	51	Ⓐ Ⓑ Ⓒ Ⓓ	71	Ⓐ Ⓑ Ⓒ Ⓓ	91	Ⓐ Ⓑ Ⓒ Ⓓ
12	Ⓐ Ⓑ Ⓒ Ⓓ	32	Ⓐ Ⓑ Ⓒ Ⓓ	52	Ⓐ Ⓑ Ⓒ Ⓓ	72	Ⓐ Ⓑ Ⓒ Ⓓ	92	Ⓐ Ⓑ Ⓒ Ⓓ
13	Ⓐ Ⓑ Ⓒ Ⓓ	33	Ⓐ Ⓑ Ⓒ Ⓓ	53	Ⓐ Ⓑ Ⓒ Ⓓ	73	Ⓐ Ⓑ Ⓒ Ⓓ	93	Ⓐ Ⓑ Ⓒ Ⓓ
14	Ⓐ Ⓑ Ⓒ Ⓓ	34	Ⓐ Ⓑ Ⓒ Ⓓ	54	Ⓐ Ⓑ Ⓒ Ⓓ	74	Ⓐ Ⓑ Ⓒ Ⓓ	94	Ⓐ Ⓑ Ⓒ Ⓓ
15	Ⓐ Ⓑ Ⓒ Ⓓ	35	Ⓐ Ⓑ Ⓒ Ⓓ	55	Ⓐ Ⓑ Ⓒ Ⓓ	75	Ⓐ Ⓑ Ⓒ Ⓓ	95	Ⓐ Ⓑ Ⓒ Ⓓ
16	Ⓐ Ⓑ Ⓒ Ⓓ	36	Ⓐ Ⓑ Ⓒ Ⓓ	56	Ⓐ Ⓑ Ⓒ Ⓓ	76	Ⓐ Ⓑ Ⓒ Ⓓ	96	Ⓐ Ⓑ Ⓒ Ⓓ
17	Ⓐ Ⓑ Ⓒ Ⓓ	37	Ⓐ Ⓑ Ⓒ Ⓓ	57	Ⓐ Ⓑ Ⓒ Ⓓ	77	Ⓐ Ⓑ Ⓒ Ⓓ	97	Ⓐ Ⓑ Ⓒ Ⓓ
18	Ⓐ Ⓑ Ⓒ Ⓓ	38	Ⓐ Ⓑ Ⓒ Ⓓ	58	Ⓐ Ⓑ Ⓒ Ⓓ	78	Ⓐ Ⓑ Ⓒ Ⓓ	98	Ⓐ Ⓑ Ⓒ Ⓓ
19	Ⓐ Ⓑ Ⓒ Ⓓ	39	Ⓐ Ⓑ Ⓒ Ⓓ	59	Ⓐ Ⓑ Ⓒ Ⓓ	79	Ⓐ Ⓑ Ⓒ Ⓓ	99	Ⓐ Ⓑ Ⓒ Ⓓ
20	Ⓐ Ⓑ Ⓒ Ⓓ	40	Ⓐ Ⓑ Ⓒ Ⓓ	60	Ⓐ Ⓑ Ⓒ Ⓓ	80	Ⓐ Ⓑ Ⓒ Ⓓ	100	Ⓐ Ⓑ Ⓒ Ⓓ

READING COMPREHENSION (Part V ~ VII)

NO.	ANSWER A B C D	NO.	ANSWER A B C D	NO.	ANSWER A B C D	NO.	ANSWER A B C D	NO.	ANSWER A B C D
101	Ⓐ Ⓑ Ⓒ Ⓓ	121	Ⓐ Ⓑ Ⓒ Ⓓ	141	Ⓐ Ⓑ Ⓒ Ⓓ	161	Ⓐ Ⓑ Ⓒ Ⓓ	181	Ⓐ Ⓑ Ⓒ Ⓓ
102	Ⓐ Ⓑ Ⓒ Ⓓ	122	Ⓐ Ⓑ Ⓒ Ⓓ	142	Ⓐ Ⓑ Ⓒ Ⓓ	162	Ⓐ Ⓑ Ⓒ Ⓓ	182	Ⓐ Ⓑ Ⓒ Ⓓ
103	Ⓐ Ⓑ Ⓒ Ⓓ	123	Ⓐ Ⓑ Ⓒ Ⓓ	143	Ⓐ Ⓑ Ⓒ Ⓓ	163	Ⓐ Ⓑ Ⓒ Ⓓ	183	Ⓐ Ⓑ Ⓒ Ⓓ
104	Ⓐ Ⓑ Ⓒ Ⓓ	124	Ⓐ Ⓑ Ⓒ Ⓓ	144	Ⓐ Ⓑ Ⓒ Ⓓ	164	Ⓐ Ⓑ Ⓒ Ⓓ	184	Ⓐ Ⓑ Ⓒ Ⓓ
105	Ⓐ Ⓑ Ⓒ Ⓓ	125	Ⓐ Ⓑ Ⓒ Ⓓ	145	Ⓐ Ⓑ Ⓒ Ⓓ	165	Ⓐ Ⓑ Ⓒ Ⓓ	185	Ⓐ Ⓑ Ⓒ Ⓓ
106	Ⓐ Ⓑ Ⓒ Ⓓ	126	Ⓐ Ⓑ Ⓒ Ⓓ	146	Ⓐ Ⓑ Ⓒ Ⓓ	166	Ⓐ Ⓑ Ⓒ Ⓓ	186	Ⓐ Ⓑ Ⓒ Ⓓ
107	Ⓐ Ⓑ Ⓒ Ⓓ	127	Ⓐ Ⓑ Ⓒ Ⓓ	147	Ⓐ Ⓑ Ⓒ Ⓓ	167	Ⓐ Ⓑ Ⓒ Ⓓ	187	Ⓐ Ⓑ Ⓒ Ⓓ
108	Ⓐ Ⓑ Ⓒ Ⓓ	128	Ⓐ Ⓑ Ⓒ Ⓓ	148	Ⓐ Ⓑ Ⓒ Ⓓ	168	Ⓐ Ⓑ Ⓒ Ⓓ	188	Ⓐ Ⓑ Ⓒ Ⓓ
109	Ⓐ Ⓑ Ⓒ Ⓓ	129	Ⓐ Ⓑ Ⓒ Ⓓ	149	Ⓐ Ⓑ Ⓒ Ⓓ	169	Ⓐ Ⓑ Ⓒ Ⓓ	189	Ⓐ Ⓑ Ⓒ Ⓓ
110	Ⓐ Ⓑ Ⓒ Ⓓ	130	Ⓐ Ⓑ Ⓒ Ⓓ	150	Ⓐ Ⓑ Ⓒ Ⓓ	170	Ⓐ Ⓑ Ⓒ Ⓓ	190	Ⓐ Ⓑ Ⓒ Ⓓ
111	Ⓐ Ⓑ Ⓒ Ⓓ	131	Ⓐ Ⓑ Ⓒ Ⓓ	151	Ⓐ Ⓑ Ⓒ Ⓓ	171	Ⓐ Ⓑ Ⓒ Ⓓ	191	Ⓐ Ⓑ Ⓒ Ⓓ
112	Ⓐ Ⓑ Ⓒ Ⓓ	132	Ⓐ Ⓑ Ⓒ Ⓓ	152	Ⓐ Ⓑ Ⓒ Ⓓ	172	Ⓐ Ⓑ Ⓒ Ⓓ	192	Ⓐ Ⓑ Ⓒ Ⓓ
113	Ⓐ Ⓑ Ⓒ Ⓓ	133	Ⓐ Ⓑ Ⓒ Ⓓ	153	Ⓐ Ⓑ Ⓒ Ⓓ	173	Ⓐ Ⓑ Ⓒ Ⓓ	193	Ⓐ Ⓑ Ⓒ Ⓓ
114	Ⓐ Ⓑ Ⓒ Ⓓ	134	Ⓐ Ⓑ Ⓒ Ⓓ	154	Ⓐ Ⓑ Ⓒ Ⓓ	174	Ⓐ Ⓑ Ⓒ Ⓓ	194	Ⓐ Ⓑ Ⓒ Ⓓ
115	Ⓐ Ⓑ Ⓒ Ⓓ	135	Ⓐ Ⓑ Ⓒ Ⓓ	155	Ⓐ Ⓑ Ⓒ Ⓓ	175	Ⓐ Ⓑ Ⓒ Ⓓ	195	Ⓐ Ⓑ Ⓒ Ⓓ
116	Ⓐ Ⓑ Ⓒ Ⓓ	136	Ⓐ Ⓑ Ⓒ Ⓓ	156	Ⓐ Ⓑ Ⓒ Ⓓ	176	Ⓐ Ⓑ Ⓒ Ⓓ	196	Ⓐ Ⓑ Ⓒ Ⓓ
117	Ⓐ Ⓑ Ⓒ Ⓓ	137	Ⓐ Ⓑ Ⓒ Ⓓ	157	Ⓐ Ⓑ Ⓒ Ⓓ	177	Ⓐ Ⓑ Ⓒ Ⓓ	197	Ⓐ Ⓑ Ⓒ Ⓓ
118	Ⓐ Ⓑ Ⓒ Ⓓ	138	Ⓐ Ⓑ Ⓒ Ⓓ	158	Ⓐ Ⓑ Ⓒ Ⓓ	178	Ⓐ Ⓑ Ⓒ Ⓓ	198	Ⓐ Ⓑ Ⓒ Ⓓ
119	Ⓐ Ⓑ Ⓒ Ⓓ	139	Ⓐ Ⓑ Ⓒ Ⓓ	159	Ⓐ Ⓑ Ⓒ Ⓓ	179	Ⓐ Ⓑ Ⓒ Ⓓ	199	Ⓐ Ⓑ Ⓒ Ⓓ
120	Ⓐ Ⓑ Ⓒ Ⓓ	140	Ⓐ Ⓑ Ⓒ Ⓓ	160	Ⓐ Ⓑ Ⓒ Ⓓ	180	Ⓐ Ⓑ Ⓒ Ⓓ	200	Ⓐ Ⓑ Ⓒ Ⓓ

DATA SHEET

PAGODA Books

※ 본 OMR 카드는 실전 연습용으로 제공되었으며,
OMR 성적 처리는 별도로 제공되지 않음을
알려드립니다.

ANSWER SHEET

PAGODA Books

문제 번호

성 명

LISTENING COMPREHENSION (Part I ~ IV)

READING COMPREHENSION (Part V ~ VII)

DATA SHEET

PAGODA Books

ANSWER SHEET

PAGODA Books

문제번호

성명

LISTENING COMPREHENSION (Part I~IV)

READING COMPREHENSION (Part V~VII)